Leverage Change

8 Ways To Achieve Faster, Easier, Better Results

Robert W. Jake Jacobs

16pt

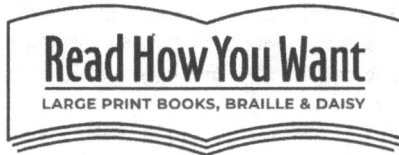

Read How You Want

LARGE PRINT BOOKS, BRAILLE & DAISY

Copyright Page from the Original Book

Leverage Change

Berrett-Koehler Publishers, Inc.
1333 Broadway, Suite 1000
Oakland, CA 94612-1921
Tel: (510) 817-2277, Fax: (510) 817-2278
www.bkconnection.com

Ordering information for print editions

Quantity sales. Special discounts are available on quantity purchases by corporations, associations, and others. For details, contact the "Special Sales Department" at the Berrett-Koehler address above.

Individual sales. Berrett-Koehler publications are available through most bookstores. They can also be ordered directly from Berrett-Koehler: Tel: (800) 929-2929; Fax: (802) 864-7626; www.bkconnection.com

Orders for college textbook/course adoption use. Please contact Berrett-Koehler: Tel: (800) 929-2929; Fax: (802) 864-7626.

Distributed to the U.S. trade and internationally by Penguin Random House Publisher Services.

Berrett-Koehler and the BK logo are registered trademarks of Berrett-Koehler Publishers, Inc.

First Edition
2021-1

Production manager: Susan Geraghty; Cover design: Rob Johnson, Toprotype, Inc.; Interior design, illustrations, and composition: Westchester Publishing Services; Copyeditor: Michele D. Jones; Proofreader: Cathy Mallon; Indexer: Carolyn Thibault; Author photo: Michael Nemeth

TABLE OF CONTENTS

TABLE OF CONTENTS

OTHER BOOKS BY ROBERT W. JAKE JACOBS

Real Time Strategic Change
You Don't Have to Do It Alone

To Mom, from whom I learned the importance of helping others.

To Dad, who taught me that optimism can be a way of life.

PREFACE

The purpose of *Leverage Change* is to make great things happen with change for individuals, teams, and organizations. You'll do this by seeing your work with a fresh lens. I call it Leverage Change. It is a new kind of change, one where using leverage will result in greater returns with fewer problems on your part. There are three ways to win with the levers. Each makes using leverage valuable with any change work, any time, any place made by anyone.

The first way to use the levers is to improve the approach you're already using. Stories in the following pages describe the levers being applied to large and small changes, simple or complex projects, newly launched efforts or those an organization has been tackling for some time. Each of these kinds of situations provides an excellent opportunity to use the levers to enhance your work.

Apply these levers, and you'll accelerate and sustain any and all change work you are doing. There's no need to radically change course, no requirement to stop doing what you've been doing. Just supplement your current work with some or all of these eight tried-and-true strategies, and you too can find your way to a world of faster, easier, better results. The 8 Levers are the counterargument to the one-best-way school of thought. They are designed to play well with others.

Currently, change methods vie for attention and a loyal following. There need be no debate about whether your current approach or the 8 Levers are a smarter path for you to pursue. The answer to this question is a resounding *yes!* Stay on the trusted path you've been traveling. Add the levers to the work you already have under way and make even more progress. Find a place where your projects and initiatives will benefit from greater speed, ease, and effectiveness, and you've found a home for the levers.

The second way you can use the 8 Levers is to apply them to achieve organization-wide change without a formal effort by applying one lever. As soon as you use a lever, change begins. Automatically, you begin the journey toward your preferred future. Choose to apply a lever sitting alone in your office, in conversation with a colleague, or in a team meeting. Use one or more of the levers to guide your thinking or your approach to a situation. Pay attention as they point you toward a small, strategic action. Watch how leverage starts moving you closer to your desired results.

Think of the 8 Levers as having a coach running alongside you as you make your way through a marathon. Open your mind to adapting how you compete in the race. Add a few straightforward strategies that lead to your running faster and better for the rest of the race, similar to adding a lever or two to your current work. No need to lose momentum or take time off the course to learn a whole newfangled way to run. Keep steaming along but with leverage, small adjustments leading to big changes. Move your arms a bit less. Lean forward as you follow the runner in front of you. In this case, doing less—but the right bit of less—improves your performance. In the case of the 8 Levers, smart changes in thought and action lead to big improvements in accomplishing the results you are seeking.

A third way to use the levers is to improve your own work, however you define it. If you're interested in getting a job done faster, more easily, and better, the levers can help you on that journey. Because the levers are scalable, what works for an organization or team can work for you too. Whether you are in the C suite or on the front line, you have tasks you need to complete. You can do them more efficiently and effectively by bringing the levers to bear on the work at hand. Know what success looks like, define the work needed to get there, apply the levers, and reap the benefits.

Who This Book Is For

This book is for CEOs, business unit leaders, functional heads, supervisors, and anyone leading a team or wanting to make changes in their own work.

Internal and external consultants and coaches charged with supporting these leaders in making change happen will also benefit from *Leverage Change*. Readers should also include trainers and educators focused on better ways to change.

Finally, anyone wanting to improve the way they work will find useful, practical counsel in these pages.

Organization of the Book and How to Read It

Chapters 1 through 8 explain the levers. Each describes a common problem with change and how that chapter's lever addresses it. This is followed by a section on how applying that particular lever leads to faster, easier, better results. This answers the question, "Why bother using the lever in the first place?" Next, you will see a list of success criteria for the lever. What do you need to have put in place to effectively use the lever? You'll also find a segment on how you know you've applied the lever well. What evidence do you have that you gained the benefits you deserve from using the lever?

There are forty-four true stories and cases included throughout the book. These introduce examples from all sorts of organizations addressing change challenges. Some involve just one person. Others tell the tale of tens of thousands of people. You'll read about organizations trying to build on a track record of success and those fighting their way out of a death spiral. These stories are meant to spark your own thinking about how you might apply the levers to advance change in your own situation.

Chapter 9 takes a step back, explaining the basics of Leverage Change—what it is, how it works, how to do it well, and what I mean by faster, easier, better results. Chapter 10 focuses on how to put the levers to work in your world. How do you select the lever with the highest likelihood of helping you toward your future? It discusses how you can pull multiple levers at the same time, both those that are more familiar and others that might be new to you. It also includes a summary of tips and advice for applying each lever.

You can either read the book from cover to cover or pick out chapters on specific levers that interest you the most. You may prefer to review the common problems at the beginning of the lever chapters and identify those getting in the way of your progress. I invite you to read the same way that you'll ultimately use the levers—the way that works best for you.

Because we're dealing with leverage, taking away even one small "aha!" from the book holds the potential of making an enormous difference in your work. My goal is for you to possess the means to tackle any tough problem you're having with change, to know which lever to use, how, and when. My colleagues and I have applied these levers in our work with organizations for more than thirty-five years. I've seen how leverage has served so many so well. Employ the levers. Expand your impact. Move your world.

INTRODUCTION

HOW TO GAIN THE MOST FROM LEVERAGE CHANGE

People struggle with change. They complain that it's hard. It takes too long. Costs too much. And, at the end of the day, is all too often ineffective. Don't take my word for it. Look at your own experience. Wouldn't you jump at the chance to achieve faster, easier, and better results?

What kind of changes am I talking about? Everything from

- Developing and implementing new strategies and cultures
- Achieving successful mergers and acquisitions
- Launching teams charged with challenging roles and responsibilities
- Resolving conflicts between different parts of your organization
- Redesigning work
- Partnering in original ways with stakeholders
- Making any change needed for you to realize your preferred future

Whether we're talking about Fortune 500 conglomerates or start-up operations, change is the challenge of the day. Leaders want to create more competitive businesses. Nonprofits and NGOs yearn for ways to increase their impact with limited resources. People want to create safer, more livable cities. Governments would love to get more done with less. Individuals strive to realize more of their potential.

Efficient and effective change is a goal we all find appealing. The number, pace, and complexity of changes bombarding us continue to rise. Increasingly integrated social networks, innovative technologies, virtual working arrangements, and multiplying customer needs all add to the demands faced by change leaders. This is also true for coaches and consultants to executives, entrepreneurs, and educators.

Wouldn't it be great if there were a systematic way to achieve faster, easier, better results?

There is. It's called Leverage Change.

Why Leverage?

Archimedes was an ancient Greek mathematician, born in 287BC. He is credited with many inventions, including explaining how and why levers work the way they do. A lever is a beam and a fixed hinge that acts as a fulcrum. Archimedes could move even the heaviest objects by putting one end of a tree branch (the lever) under the heavy object, moving a smaller rock (the fulcrum) under the beam, and finally, at the other end, pushing down on the beam (see Figure I.1).

If Archimedes ever joined a contest for moving heavy objects, he would win. The lever was his secret weapon, one that gave him superhuman strength. The strongest man in the world could push the heavy object with all the power he had, but never budge it. Archimedes, however, could walk up to the object, put his lever in place, push down on it, and, like magic, the object would move. The competition was over, Archimedes the victor.

.

Here's a quick physics lesson. Leverage is the compounding force gained by the use of a lever rotating on a fulcrum. Archimedes gained an extraordinary increase in power with relatively little investment needed. Despite having fewer resources to invest (his lesser strength), he succeeded where others failed. The leverage he gained from using the right tools made the impossible possible. The closer to the boulder he put the pivot, the more leverage he gained. The more leverage he gained, the easier the weight was to move.

FIGURE I.1. "Give me a lever long enough and a fulcrum on which to place it, and I shall move the world."—Archimedes

Archimedes found an alternative to sheer manpower, and because of his insight, he was able to accomplish what others could not. Fortunately, we can take advantage of Archimedes's insight today. We can apply the concept of leverage to the world of change.

With a long-enough lever and a fulcrum on which to pivot it, anyone can move their world. That is the essence of leverage: take smart, strategic actions and generate large, positive impact. Your change efforts will achieve faster, easier, and better results than you imagined when you apply the power of leverage to your work.

What Is Leverage Change?

Leverage Change is a new way to look at the age-old challenge of how to succeed in organization change. At its core, this approach asks a simple yet profound question: How can you make changes taking full advantage of the power and possibilities that come with the concept of leverage? Leverage accelerates the pace at which you move into your future. It lightens your load along the way. Your change work becomes more successful. How do you do this?

Consider four elements. The first is the levers. These are akin to Archimedes's log. Their length is commensurate with their impact. High-impact levers are long ones. I offer eight of these in this book. They are proven ways to gain faster, easier, better results on any kind of change, any place, at any time made by anyone. They act as turbochargers to your efforts, improving the good work you're already doing. They also help shore up areas where you're coming up short of the mark.

The second element is the resources you allocate. Resources can be any combination of time, money, energy, and talent you devote to your change work. For example, they could be political capital, leadership competencies, or funds to invest in new technology. The more leverage you gain, the fewer hassles, headaches, and problems you experience.

The third element, the pivot point in the world of Leverage Change, is set based on how clear you are about the results you desire. The more clarity you have about your desired results, the closer the fulcrum sits to the object (see Figure I.2). More clarity equals greater leverage working for you. Greater leverage means more power to do the work you desire.

The less clear you are about the results you desire, the further away your fulcrum point sits from these results. In this situation, leverage works against you (see Figure I.3). It would be much harder for Archimedes to lift his heavy object, or for you to achieve your desired results, with the fulcrum further away from your preferred end state.

The fourth element is making sure that you're moving the *right* heavy object. The "rightness" of your desired results matters. A lot. Changing in ways that are faster, easier, and better toward the wrong results will only sink your ship sooner, with less effort and more effectively.

Remember that you are applying the power of a simple machine, the lever, to the complexity inherent in organizations. Do so well, and you can get the energy in your organization working for you instead of against you. There are so many variables involved in organization change that trying to keep track of them all is a tall order. Here's a new goal: leverage the wisdom, experience, and people in your organization to achieve results that you desire.

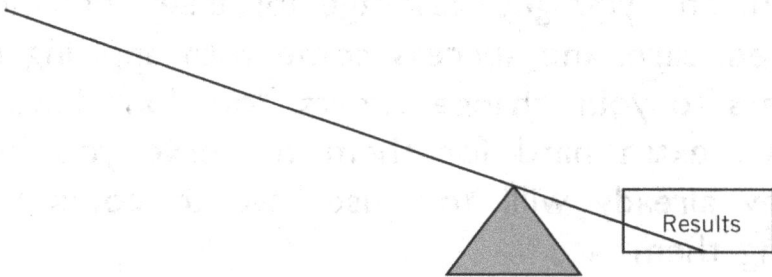

The clearer the desired results, the closer you are to achieving them. FIGURE I.2. Leverage Working for You

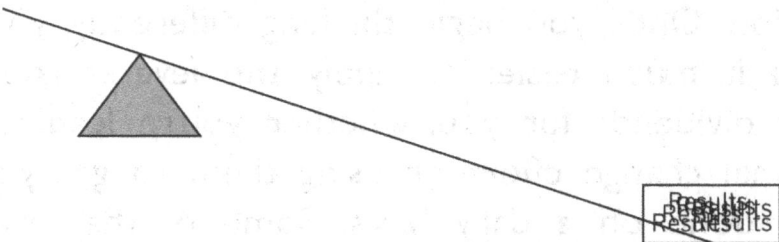

The fuzzier and more confusing the desired results, the further away you are to achieving them. FIGURE I.3 Leverage Working against You

Stuart Kauffman, a leading voice in the field of complexity science, has stated that you get "order for free" in the universe.[1] He argues that there is an underlying order to life itself. We don't have to work to cause the world and the organizations in it to make sense. With careful observation, we can recognize that they already do. There are patterns that can be understood and used to guide your change work. The levers work in much the same way. Use them and you get "leverage for free." Enhanced speed, ease, and success come with applying the levers to your change efforts. You don't have to work extra hard for them to serve you well. They already will. You just have to commit to using them.

What Are the 8 Levers?

A lever is both a mindset and a guide for action. Once you begin thinking differently, you'll find it much easier to apply the levers. They'll pay dividends for you, whether you're leading a formal change effort or using them to get your job done on a daily basis. Some of the levers may be familiar to you. Perhaps you already use them to your advantage. Others could be approaches you've never imagined before. Try them all. Experiment with them in different situations and with different people. They are incredibly flexible.

The more needed levers you apply, the faster, easier, and better your change work occurs. Think of keeping the lever or levers that will make the greatest positive influence in your situation front and center. Make sure you apply these well. Some will give you greater impact at a particular time. Others will make a bigger difference during another phase of your work. A single lever on its own may make the difference needed at one time. Sometimes you may decide that's all you need. At others, two, three, four, or more levers can be your right choice. The more you work with them, the better you'll be able to get them working for you.

THE 8 LEVERS OF LEVERAGE CHANGE

- **Pay Attention to Continuity**

    This first lever asks you to take a paradoxical approach to your challenge. Champion continuity, and you'll soon be celebrating successful change.

- **Think and Act as If the Future Were Now!**

    Make your preferred future real today, not something that you talk about or envision for a later time. Live tomorrow, today. Increased ownership, accelerated change, and decreased resistance will soon follow.

- **Design It Yourself**

  Each organization has unique challenges and opportunities. These have to be factored into the purpose and design of its change effort. You need to chart your own course of action, not follow someone else's.

- **Create a Common Database**

  Each member of an organization makes decisions every day that have an impact on the future direction and results of the entire enterprise. No matter their size, these decisions all count. The more informed and aligned they are, the more successful you will be.

- **Start with Impact, Follow the Energy**

  Decide where to begin your work based on opportunities for impact. The organizational energy you generate will point the way toward future progress. Change work needs to evolve based on people's readiness, needs, and desires.

- **Develop a Future People Want to Call Their Own**

  Effective change is defined by success for each individual, each team, the organization as a whole, and key stakeholders. It's not enough for some to win and others to lose. Commitment comes from creating a future that all involved want to call their own.

- **Find Opportunities for People to Make a Meaningful Difference**

  People in organizations have their regular job. Formal change efforts create unique possibilities for people to make a meaningful difference in their organization's future. Discover these opportunities and make the most of them, for each individual and the common good.

- **Make Change Work Part of Daily Work**

  Change is constant in organizations. With this lever, change can occur outside formal change efforts. Innovation, new markets, and better ways of working come to those who don't separate this kind of informal change work from daily work. In these cases, change is part of everyone's job. Every day.

How Can You Use the Levers?

The levers can help you in three ways, each with its own benefits and set of circumstances.

Way to Apply the Levers 1: To Further Improve a Formal Change Program

Resistance is a natural consequence of creating a formal change program. You're purposefully trying to make something different. Some people will quickly and enthusiastically get on board with new ways of doing business. Others will wait to see how things pan out before making a commitment. Then there's that third group—the people who for whatever reason don't agree with the proposed change and dedicate themselves to preserving the status quo.

This dynamic plays out to some degree even in the most inclusive change approaches. More recent methods heavy on involvement minimize it, but anyone who claims they have a way to bring about change with zero resistance is, I believe, telling a tall tale. We'll get into more detail on all 8 Levers throughout the rest of the book. For now, let's look more concretely at one of them to illustrate how the levers can make a good thing even better.

The lever highlighted in the following story is Design It Yourself. It demonstrates how to resolve the issue of people resisting a change approach because it was "Not Invented Here."

People tend to resist approaches that are not homegrown. These approaches come from outside the organization and get labeled as foreign bodies; they are a perfect setup for those looking for something to resist.

STORY

The first day we began working within a telecommunications company, we experienced the power of the "Not Invented Here" mantra. Joe, a member of the cross-sectional group crafting plans for their organization's change effort, stood in the doorway the entire morning of our first day together. He served as a physical manifestation of a metaphor—he literally kept two feet outside the change process. When asked why he refused to take a seat at the table with the rest of the team, he replied, "I've seen this happen too many times."

He explained that the organization's MO was for someone on the executive team to decide that some big change was needed and then it was rolled out across the whole business. "Better said," he continued, "they roll it *over* the organization, flattening anything and anybody in its way. Then these same leaders complain that we're behind the implementation schedule, quality's suffering, current production's been negatively impacted, and there's a whole host of other problems we get blamed for." He concluded by saying he had nothing more to say. He folded his arms in front of himself with a quiet snort.

We devoted the morning session to a brief overview of the planning team's role and our Leverage Change approach of Design It Yourself that meant the team would be defining the purpose, outcomes, and road map for their own change effort. We then moved on to understand people's experience of the organization's past and hopes for the future. Each person had an opportunity to share their thoughts and feelings. Some themes emerged and disagreements arose. Every perspective was valued as we explained that these were all pieces of the larger jigsaw puzzle called reality. The afternoon would be spent digging in to begin creating the organization's own change process.

At lunch, Joe grabbed a sandwich and sat down next to me. I asked him what he thought of the morning's work. Joe's comment: "This feels different to me. Everybody's listening to one another, even the higher-ups. I know we need to transform the business and make changes to stay competitive. That's just life. But having us figure out for ourselves how we're going to go about it ... now that's different. I'm in." I smiled and welcomed Joe aboard the team.

How many Joes—good people who care, but who over time have become jaded by negative past experiences—do you have in your organization? When have you had a predetermined program rolled out in the organization (or rolled over people, as Joe put it) without regard to its impact?

As is often the case with the strongest cynics in change situations, once they come to appreciate a sincere effort to engage people in the organization, they become equally strong supporters. Joe later led a group of informal leaders who championed the change effort, made a video describing its benefits, and invited every colleague to join him on this team.

Way to Apply the Levers 2: To Create Organization-Wide Change by Applying One Lever

Think of having a string of dominoes lined up for you. You need only tap the first one to hear the click, click, click of a cascade of pieces falling in a sequence of intricate patterns no matter how long the line. Little effort is needed to get the entire process going. Gravity does the rest.

The levers work in much the same way. A single lever, appropriately applied, can lead to far-reaching changes across your entire organization. Select a situation where change is needed. Identify which lever may be the most promising and let it guide your thinking and approach. You can do this by

- Identifying which lever intrigues you the most—do any capture your curiosity?
- Following your gut—which seems likely to have the most impact?
- Conducting a short experiment—what immediate impact do you experience from applying one of the levers?

Pay attention as your chosen lever or levers point you toward a small, strategic action. Watch how leverage starts working for you and your organization as you begin moving toward your desired future. Expend little effort. The lever does the rest.

The lever spotlighted in the following story is Pay Attention to Continuity. This lever reminds us not to get too caught up thinking about, talking about, and working only on change to the relative exclusion of continuity. It counsels us to also build support for our efforts by focusing on preserving what you do well as you make needed changes.

STORY

A retail company was eager to extend its footprint into Europe ahead of competitors. The whole company was focused on a rapid growth strategy. As much as the CEO wanted to move the organization forward quickly, he realized that there was gold to be mined from the past. Move too fast in implementing new ways of doing business, and you can inadvertently take your eye off the ball in terms of important contributors to earlier success.

Once introduced to the Pay Attention to Continuity lever, the CEO made sure to ask questions in meetings with his direct reports, of others in the organization, and during individual conversations. These inquiries expanded daily talks by emphasizing the importance of both continuity and change in creating the business's future. He invited people to explore how the company could stay on track with the current business while making changes needed to build new markets. What kind of leadership had been cultivated in the past that would serve the organization well with the new growth strategy? What other skills and abilities would be needed for success in the future?

Applying this one lever made a big difference. The CEO's new continuity paradigm expanded as did those of others with whom he interacted in the organization. The change agenda remained an essential priority in achieving the new strategy, but not the only one. Pairing this clear priority with the less obvious one of ensuring that enough attention was paid to continuity made the path to success faster, easier, and better than it otherwise would have been.

Way to Apply the Levers 3: To Achieve Faster, Easier, Better Results in Any Work You Do

The 8 Levers described in this book are for anyone interested in achieving faster, easier, better results. As I've said, they are shortcuts to succeeding in making any change, anywhere, anytime, and by anyone—from the CEO to a frontline worker. Think of them as core competencies for the twenty-first-century organization and its members.

Easily taught, they can be applied equally well by people with deep expertise in change and those just getting started. Whether you're engaged in an organization-wide effort or a team initiative, or in improving your own work, the levers are for you. The third way to apply the levers is to use them in any situation in which work is being done. Wondering how to shorten the time needed for you to build trust with a colleague? Wish you could make it easier to get people to complete expense reports by the deadline? Looking for ways to raise the quality of interactions with your boss? The levers can help in every one of these situations.

STORY

A client of mine was once lamenting the trouble he was having getting a new hire up to speed. When he first brought her on board, he had high hopes about the value she could add, but things just weren't working out that way. He wasn't able to put his finger on the issue, but was growing impatient. The two of them had already had a couple of meetings about expectations to iron things out, but the new hire's work was still not up to par. Things were starting to come to a head—his team was now complaining—and he began consulting with his own boss about whether to keep the new hire or begin a search for a better fit.

It was then that I suggested he apply the Think and Act as If the Future Were Now! lever. I explained to him that this meant he could no longer look at this new hire as the subpar performer she had been. He needed to think and act as if this till-now perceived problem was his new Most Valuable Player. This powerful approach is counterintuitive. I was asking him to see his biggest problem as its own solution.

He looked at me bewildered, shook his head, and said he was ready to try anything to avoid starting the hiring process again. Over the next few weeks, he treated her as a highly valued team member, one with good ideas that could benefit the team and even the entire organization. He listened to her counsel as he would that of a trusted advisor and encouraged the team to partner with her as though she held the key to solving some of their most vexing problems.

When I checked in on my client a few weeks later, he had an entirely different story to tell me about this woman. He found she actually did have some very good ideas. The team warmed to her and gained some insights into those thorny issues they'd been wrestling with for some time.

By using the lever Think and Act as If the Future Were Now!, my client had actually created his desired future. He had envisioned what he wanted and began to behave as if he already had it. That's the power of one person using the levers to improve their own situation and, in doing so, adding value for the organization as well. I'm not saying every new problem employee will work out well by applying a lever to their situation. But using a lever wisely, as my client did, will help you create your preferred future more often than you'd believe.

Succeeding or Struggling? It Doesn't Matter

Your change work to date may be something to write home about. You could be ahead of schedule, under budget, and well supported in your efforts. Or maybe your work has been mostly effective. You're getting the job done. People feel pretty good about the work they've been doing, but there's room for improvement. Or perhaps you fall into a third category: You're struggling. You're missing milestones. Frustration is mounting. You see no clear way out of the mess.

Regardless of which of these describes your current situation, the 8 Levers can help you. *Faster, easier,* and *better* are relative terms. Faster, easier, and better than what? Than what you would otherwise believe possible. What looks like progress for you might be unacceptable to another, or vice versa. Using the levers is like putting an accelerator on your change effort. You'll gain the advantage of leverage by following the recommendations in this book. Progress will come more easily. Positive momentum will be on your side. You'll need less effort and achieve better results. A win all the way around.

Why This Book Matters

I've written two books previous to this one. Both are about how to involve people in formal organization change efforts of one type or another. Over time, I've gotten a reputation as an "involvement guy." I was one of the pioneers in the field of large group interventions. My colleagues and I have brought hundreds and even thousands of people together at the same time and place to address real issues in real time. I still believe involvement is an important element to successful organization change. But not the only important one. And in some cases, maybe not even the best one for your situation.

All-or-nothing thinking takes over when people debate the best way for organizations to change. "My way is right—that means yours has to be wrong." Those following each school of thought carry their own flag. Instead of believing there is one best way, this book argues for a "many best ways" paradigm. The best way is the one that works for you and your organization, given your past experience, current capabilities, future needs, and many more factors. Organization change is too complex to boil down to a single approach as the end-all, be-all answer.

That's where the levers come into play. They provide the flexibility needed in the real world. Sometimes, involvement is a good approach. At other times, direction will serve you better. Some situations call for starting change efforts at the top of the organization. In other cases, you'll make more progress by starting where you can create the biggest impact.

Improvements for individuals, teams, and organizations can also occur without chartering a change group, launching a new initiative, or creating a formal change effort. This book, and the levers, answer the question of how that is possible. Wouldn't it be great if you could bring about widespread change with a simple shift in mindset or a single act? That's what applying one lever looks like at work in your world.

Expect the unexpected as you read on. Common change problems get solved with the uncommon wisdom of the levers. Change is what this whole book is about, but the first lever described urges you to pay extra attention to continuity. The most straightforward way to use the levers? Identify the common problem you're facing. Select your lever. Apply it. Solve the problem. It really is that easy to get it right.

Getting it right means leaving it to you to design, manage, and lead your own change work. The levers will help you along that path. You decide on your route forward. Stumbling along the way? Things not going according to plan? Pause and reflect. What problem are you facing? Lacking support? Go to the Design It Yourself lever. People not informed enough to make good decisions? Look to the Create a Common Database lever. As you read on, you'll become more familiar with the levers and which common problems they address. You're sure to recognize the problems. We've all experienced them. The levers give you a set of tried-and-true remedies for these struggles.

Read on. Use the levers that make sense for your situation. Leave the rest alone—for now. Eventually you'll find that different levers fit different scenarios. The following pages offer plenty of examples of applying the levers in a wide variety of situations involving all sorts of changes in all kinds of organizations. Go forth and move your world!

I

PAY ATTENTION TO CONTINUITY

Change, change, change. It's all you hear about. When it's time for organization change, banners are unfurled, communications teams go into overdrive, leaders ready their stump speeches. The promise of a better, more exciting future and healthier culture lies ahead. The company will be more competitive in the marketplace. Smarter ways of working will take hold. Everyone will be pulling together toward a common cause. Assurances are made. Resources are devoted to making things different. Confidence is stoked and enthusiasm encouraged. Momentum builds ... until it doesn't. All the hype, pomp, and circumstance run into the buzz saw of reality. Resistance mounts. People complain about wanting to return to the "good old days." New ways of working fall by the wayside. The organization regresses to business as usual. Time marches on.

A Common Problem: There's Too Much Change

Extraordinary amounts of time and care go into crafting "cases for change." All the reasons get listed in compelling detail. The arguments are persuasive. The language is crafted just so, meant to further motivate those already on the bandwagon and convince fence-sitters to come along. Common wisdom says not to focus on the strongest in opposition. They aren't likely to get on board anyway, and you don't want to waste precious resources. People are encouraged to identify the various changes required to make the effort successful. The spotlight is focused on what will be new and different. The change campaign is under way.

Sometimes this approach works. Often it does not. Why is this so often the case?

Solution: Pay Attention to Continuity

A major reason most change work falls short is that you're dealing with only half of reality. Whether people realize it consciously or not, they know there's something wrong with this picture. You're clapping with only one hand. What about a rousing chorus for a "case for continuity," highlighting all those things from the past and present that need to be part of your organization's successful future? The firmer the ground people stand on, the more able they are to push off in their leap into an uncertain future. Radical continuity makes radical change possible. Welcome to the world of paradoxical change. If you want change, don't (just) go after change. Remember and celebrate the importance of continuity, and you'll be well on your way to achieving successful change.

My friend and colleague Barry Johnson has studied and taught the concepts of paradoxical change for more than forty years.[2] His original and still growing body of knowledge is the foundation for this chapter. He views the power and possibilities of paradoxical change through a lens he calls Polarity Thinking™. Polarities are opposites that need each other over time to succeed. Take breathing as an example—inhaling and exhaling. Consider activity and rest. Both contribute to a healthy, balanced life. Organizations wrestle with all kinds of polarities every day. Do we focus on our business unit's success or on the entire enterprise's fortunes? Would we be better off centralizing shared services for efficiencies or decentralizing them to get closer to the customer? Is it smarter to go after profit today or potential for tomorrow? The best answer to all these questions is yes.

Approaching change from a paradoxical point of view transforms your greatest resisters into your staunchest allies. We know how to deal with resisters in a traditional approach to change: leave them behind. They'll either go quietly or get louder. Neither reaction is productive for moving the ball down the field. Push on them to change their views, and they push back even harder. Not only despite your best efforts but in fact because of them.

The rules of the game change when you're dealing with paradoxes and polarities. Instead of outvoting the minority, understand that the fewer the people who share a point of view and the less powerful they are, the *more you need to listen to them*. What they see and believe, others don't. Their being the minority doesn't make them wrong. It makes them even more valuable potential contributors. Rethink what these resisters have to offer. In many cases, they see traps that you can overlook in your excitement to move forward. Within a polarity paradigm, there is wisdom in resistance. It's not an obstacle to be overcome or gotten around on the way to an exciting future. It's a point of view that you need to include to get to that exciting future.

People with an "Or" mindset get stuck in useless debates about whether the organization needs to focus on change or on continuity. Will things be better in the future because we decide to do things differently, or should we stick with the tried-and-true practices that have gotten us to where we are today? The answer to this question is a firm yes. Each of these groups is right. The problem is that each is only half right. You only get the complete answer by coming from an "And" point of view. Both continuity and change are needed for either to be successful.

Challenge your existing assumptions about what makes for successful change. Adopt a paradoxical approach and be prepared to be surprised by the ease, speed, and quality with which your efforts move forward. It's the first of our 8 Levers because it sets a context for the rest. Leverage means getting more done with less. Less resistance. Less time. Less wasted energy. A paradoxical approach to change is your first step on that journey.

STORY

An administrators' group in a health care system had been at odds with their physician colleagues for quite a while. There was a long list of items on which they disagreed: in-room treatment protocols, responsiveness to on-call paging, and documentation of patient care, to name just a few. We decided that introducing paradoxical change could break the logjam between the two groups. We introduced an activity Barry has developed called the Point of View.[3] The administrators were charged with representing the "continuity" point of view; the physicians, the "change" perspective.

Each group was given the same assignment to prepare for the conversation they were going to have: identify all the benefits of your argument and the costs of overfocusing on the other group's preference. Then we brought four administrators to one side of the round tables we'd set up and four doctors to the other. Their goal? Convince the other side that their position was the right course of action for the hospital to follow. The energy in the room skyrocketed straight away. The conversations got louder and more animated the longer they continued. We listened in on one table group.

Administrators: We've had great test scores ten years running from the Joint Commission (an accreditation organization for health care systems). Why change something that's not broken!

Doctors: There are new practices being developed all over the world. We should be learning and taking advantage of the latest innovations on behalf of our patients.

The benefits of each side saw the light of day.

Doctors: Sure, what we did in the past led to high rankings, but those great scores from yesterday do nothing to assure solid marks tomorrow!

Administrators: Some of those new approaches haven't even gone through rigorous testing, and we agreed that evidence-based medicine was all that we would practice in this institution.

Both made good points about the risks of overfocusing on one point of view to the relative exclusion of the other.

Although this activity was introduced as a role play, some of these points hit home. Neither group disagreed with what the other had said. It just wasn't in the forefront of their minds. The doctors and administrators looked at each other kind of sheepishly. Some of the points raised had been actual arguments the two groups had made to each other previously.

Paradoxical change pointed out the wisdom in both perspectives. Everyone was affirmed.

The whole group found something everyone cared about: excellent patient care. The two groups had a fresh perspective on their prior conflict. Each side had something to contribute, and each had something to gain from the other. Sometimes being right isn't enough when you represent only half of reality.

How This Lever Helps Create Faster, Easier, Better Results

The Pay Attention to Continuity lever leads to new thoughts and behaviors. You move from defining the people who are resisting change as problems to creating an expanded team where everyone's voice is heard. You want to use this lever in your change work for the following five reasons:

1. *This lever reduces resistance to change from those valuing continuity.* The greater the resistance, the slower your change. People may argue that there are methods that have served them well in the past. Great. What were they, and will they help us move toward our preferred future? Others extol the virtues of parts of the culture they don't want to lose. Super. Let's identify and

preserve the aspects that will work going forward. You'll hear arguments that even though roles are changing, key performance indicators for the institution should stay the same. Exactly. What's worked before can work again. Even when people are holding on to outdated practices that won't serve them well in the future, listen. Dig deeper to understand why they're still holding on. Resist the urge to dismiss them. You'll be wiser about why things haven't worked and have less resistance pushing against you.

2. *It ensures that you benefit from past practices that will serve you well in the future.* There are plenty of ways you've worked in the past that have been effective. You're never starting from scratch when it comes to change. The difference is that this time you're making no assumptions. Consciously pay attention to what's gone well in the past and be sure to bring it forward into the future. Don't leave it to chance that these points will be made. Identify anything and everything from the past that has been successful. Let nothing get lost in the shuffle. What's worked is good for your future. What needs to change can lead to even better solutions. Take your pick of the most important aspects that need to

be retained in your situation and emphasize them. Here's a starter list to consider:

- Teams that work together
- Where they work
- Tools they use
- Groups with whom they interact
- Customers they serve
- Suppliers they partner with

The possibilities go on and on. Next time someone talks to you about a big change, be smart enough to also ask about the big things that will continue just as they have from the past.

3. *You're clear and strategic about what to continue from your past.* When you're clear about what you want to continue from the past, you'll build a more accurate list of what you need to change. Typically, people decide what to change. What doesn't make the list ends up staying the same. This isn't a conscious or considered process. Give as much time and attention to what you're going to continue doing as to what you'll be doing in new ways. What you continue from the past will have as much impact on your future success as what you decide to change.

4. *You build one large organization-wide team valuing both continuity and change.* No one

gets left off this team. Everyone is valued for their unique perspective. Some people will be natural traditionalists and favor the best of the past and present. Others will inherently focus on innovation, always on the lookout for new and better ways of working. These two camps need to get used to getting along. Their battles have likely been waged for years. Adopting a paradoxical approach to change eliminates conflict between the two groups. Neither is "right" or "wrong."

5. *You stand the best chance of achieving your ultimate purpose.* Regardless of what you are trying to accomplish, you'll be worse off for not applying this lever. Continuity and change each brings its own engine to creating your future. Pay attention to only one, and you're working with half the power you have available. Doing a good job on change and dropping a few balls on the continuity side of the equation will cost you dearly. Without careful and consistent attention to both continuity and change, you'll sell yourself and your organization short. Customers will be disappointed. Quality numbers will suffer. Financial forecasts will fall short of the mark.

Success Factors in Applying This Lever

A paradoxical approach requires new assumptions and beliefs. Make changes to your own paradigm, and you can lead others down a similarly helpful path. The success factors that follow are the rules of the road for this new world of possibilities.

Factor One: Adopt a Paradoxical Point of View about Change

You have to see change for what it is—half the equation. Going after change to create more change ... will create less. You'll build your own resistance. People getting in the way of your grand change efforts have made your job harder since day 1, putting up roadblocks that slow your best efforts. Maybe it's you who's had it wrong all along.

Once you see change paradoxically, you can never see it another way again. Leverage is not found in pushing harder, arguing louder, or holding on to your position longer. There's a new set of rules to follow. Seek out the old guard and have them tell you stories of the good old days. Let go of your beliefs about these folks being past their expiration date, out of touch, and behind the times. Assume instead that they are your best friends, bringing nuggets of wisdom to the table—nuggets you would have stumbled past on your way to a bigger and brighter future.

Factor Two: Believe That There Is Wisdom in Resistance

To make this lever work for you, you have to sincerely bring this belief on board. People will know if you're faking it. We all have internal BS radar. Make a commitment to see the world differently. Give yourself a challenge. See whether you can identify the wisdom being shared in the resistance you're hearing. Learn to say, "Could you say more?" to encourage so-called resisters to feel safe enough to share the mother lode of insight they possess. Trust them, and they will begin to trust you.

Factor Three: Commit to Listening to the Fewer and Less Powerful

If you can make this commitment, you'll be more than halfway home. We're used to taking a vote and letting the majority rule, or having the boss make the call. In the world of paradoxical change, both of these approaches will put you on a path of pain. With enough hierarchical power, you can push your agenda forward against the greatest of odds. Instead, take a more productive approach. Shine a spotlight on minority points of view. Give them equal airtime. Create a culture where smaller bands of believers speak with larger megaphones. You already know who these people are in your organization. Seek them out. Tell them you want to hear from them. Create opportunities in meetings for them to share their perspectives. Encourage others to appreciate the paradoxical approach to change—and the unique value brought by these outliers to the organization's norms. Make a commitment to do this, to yourself and for the organization.

Factor Four: See Those Resisting Change as Key Contributors, Not Troublemakers

This success factor asks that you shift your mindset and emotions around those who have resisted change. In your quiet moments of contemplation, you may have wondered, *What will it take to get these people to move on and bother another organization with their pessimistic points of view?* I'm asking you to change your tune about them. They are, and always have been, key contributors to your cause. You just haven't seen them that way. Every time you saw them causing trouble, they were trying to do what's best for the organization. As my colleagues and I once said in an earlier book, *You Don't Have to Do It Alone: How to Involve Others to Get Things Done*, "Troublemaking is in the eye of the beholder."[4] See them as troublemakers, and you'll have trouble on your hands. Choose to view them as key contributors, and you'll wonder how you ever got along without them.

Factor Five: Know That You're All on the Same Team

There's no longer an "us vs. them" game to play. That's been an unhelpful assumption since the day you adopted it. Tap into the power of your organization-wide team, and you'll ride your wave of change (and continuity) into the future you desire. Having people fighting between continuity and change in your organization can be exhausting. People are tired. They've kept putting forth their best efforts, only to be thwarted by their colleagues doing the very same thing from another perspective. When you get all the energy in your organization working for you, it's like paddling downstream. The current makes it easier, not harder, to achieve progress. You cover twice the distance with half the effort. It's the best way to travel.

STORY

Many paradoxes, or polarities, in challenging change efforts can be seen through the lens of continuity and change. Take, for example, a technology products company we worked with that was trying to implement a matrix organizational structure. The "old way" of doing business was represented by straight-line relationships in the structure. Finance, HR, quality, sales, and other functions reported directly to business unit leaders. But they also had dotted-line (read: "new ways") or indirect relationships with their functional heads, who oversaw operations for the entire company.

The matrix was new. As expected, this is what the organization was championing as part of its main change work. All-hands meetings, leadership development courses, and cascading communication gatherings were geared to what was new and different. Predictably, all this activity was creating more and more resistance to the desired shift in structure. The harder you push on a paradox, the harder it pushes back. How do you deal with this challenge?

Use something Barry calls the Getting Unstuck process.[5]

Step 1: Instead of trying to convince others of the wisdom of your argument for change, begin first by asking them why they care about continuity. What are the benefits of keeping some things the way they've been?

With this organization, we paid more attention to continuity early on. We celebrated successes from the past and called out advantages brought by the straight-line relationships, such as bringing support for services closer to the business and faster response times for customers.

Step 2: Ask them to describe concerns they have about the changes you're proposing. You'll find you'll be hard pressed in most cases to even disagree with what others say.

In this case, we asked the group to identify risks in moving to the dotted-line design; these included a loss of strong business unit teams as allegiances were now split between the business and functions. We were careful not to ignore or discount changes that needed to be made. At the same time, we didn't start by trying to proselytize to the masses about them.

Step 3: Once others know you've heard them, raise the benefits of the changes you're proposing. People are much more willing to listen once they themselves have been heard.

After highlighting the benefits of how things had been and the potential price to be paid by moving to the new plan, those involved in the change made a list of the benefits of the matrix approach. An important point they noted was that the dotted-line connections would ensure that best practices were shared across business units. The compilation of business-by-business results would also be easier to pull together at month-end.

Step 4: Double back to reaffirming the value of the past and present that they've identified. Without this step, people may feel as though you're "pulling a fast one" on them, seducing them into believing you care about their opinions, only to ignore them at the end of the day.

It was now time to confirm the value of those old straight-line relationships one more time.

Step 5: After you've convinced those resisting that you have no tricks up your sleeve, finish by reinforcing a goal you both share, be it the organization's long-term success or something else you can both agree is worth achieving.

Finally, we reminded everyone of the ultimate goal: a winning business in the marketplace. This client used the Getting Unstuck model to guide their efforts in communications, meetings, and large group events.

Don't discount the past or try to move away from it too quickly. There is gold to be mined. Grab a pickaxe and start digging. This story was about solid lines and dotted lines. Yours will be different. Remember the key words regardless of your circumstances: continuity and change. The same dynamic plays out time and again in organizations, just by different names.

How to Know You've Applied This Lever Well

Once you've put the success factors in place, a critical question remains: How well have you applied this lever? Here's a short list of items you can review to ensure that you're taking advantage of the benefits this lever has to offer in your quest for faster, easier, better results.

Previous "Resisters" and "Troublemakers" Are Celebrated as Valuable Contributors

It's one thing to tolerate resisters and troublemakers, but much harder to celebrate them. They were the Eeyores of *Winnie the Pooh* fame, moping around the organization waiting for the next bad thing to happen. Now they have become change heroes. The more you encourage people with minority viewpoints to speak up, the more successful your change work will become. The first celebration you hold for a former troublemaker is sure to shake things up. You'll have everyone's attention when you explain your new paradigm about paradoxical change. Make friends with your former foes.

Other Polarities in the Organization Are Identified and Leveraged

Continuity/Change is one polarity, an essential one when talking about paradoxical change. There are many people in your organization unnecessarily suffering through endless Or debates about And situations. These conflicts would be much more effectively approached as polarities. How can you tell you are dealing with a polarity?

If the argument is about moving from some place you currently are to another, better place in the future, you're in polarity land. From decentralized to centralized, short term to long term, operations focus to customer focus. You'll know you're applying this lever well when you hear talk in meetings about whether people are wrestling with an And polarity or an Or problem. The more you and others see and take advantage of polarities in your organization, the more certain you are of success with this lever.

People Don't Feel That They've Been Overrun or Ralroaded into Change

Ever heard the saying, "Lead, follow, or get out of the way!"? A popular battle cry for changemakers ... just not for the effective ones. Your intention may not be to steamroll people on the way to your exciting future. That doesn't matter. Their perception is your reality. Once you flatten a potential teammate, they're less likely to partner with you, regardless of the number of apologies you make as you pick them up and dust them off. If you're excited by this paradoxical change approach, don't fall into the trap of trying to immediately convince everyone of your newfound wisdom. You get no points for understanding polarities and acting like "it's my way or the highway."

You Can Point to Best Past and Present Practices That Are Thriving in the Future

Not everything from your past makes sense to bring with you into the future. However, if you find nothing worth moving forward, you've got a problem. You ought to be able to highlight past ways of doing business that have survived your change work. Creating stop-start-continue lists is one variation of this approach. Capturing working and not-working items in a small group is another. You may decide you need a more comprehensive assessment of past performance. The goal is to be clear about what's going to stay the same. Get on the paradoxical path and make it easier to get from point A to point B.

Whenever Change Is Talked About, So Is Continuity

This may be a tough one. We're so used to talking change. Continuity is much less popular. It's certainly less sexy than change. No CEO is getting on the cover of *Fortune* magazine under the headline, "We're going to keep doing what we're doing!" We live in a culture of change. There's a continually increasing rate of change in technology, customer needs, innovation, and other areas. Leaders and "change agents" are drawn to the concept like moths to a flame. For good reason. The saying "Change or die" is true. From a paradoxical point of view, though, we know that it's only half true. The less popular coffee mug slogan? "Continue or die."

Examples of This Lever in Action

Two radically different examples of the Pay Attention to Continuity lever follow: a retail company in a race to garner market share and multiple stakeholders resolving issues surrounding citywide child-care programs. Here we'll read about the flexibility of the levers. The first story highlights evidence that this lever has taken hold because other polarities in the organization are being identified and leveraged. The second points to the importance of appreciating that continuity for one group may be experienced as change by another. Read on and learn how paradoxical change made a critical contribution to each situation.

STORY: A CONSUMER PRODUCTS COMPANY MAKES USE OF "AND" THINKING

A CEO we worked with was focused intensely on accountability. Production and sales goals were going to be tough for the business to meet. Who had accountability for specific tasks along the critical path to success? How would success be measured? What were the consequences of not delivering? The CEO was frustrated because people were dropping balls left and right.

From a paradoxical point of view, the answer was obvious. We asked, "With all this focus on accountability, how much support is being provided for these people so that they can effectively fulfill their accountabilities?" The CEO looked curious. It was a question he had never considered. He immediately applied this new line of thinking in the next meeting with his direct reports by asking how he could better support them. The team expanded ownership of key actions, and those actions became shared responsibilities.

Then other parts of the organization got involved. Production and sales teams met to make new agreements on roles. They were originally planning to use a standard RACI

(Responsible, Accountable, Consult, Inform) chart to define accountabilities for specific tasks. With this insight from the CEO, they created a newfangled RASCI chart (adding in a Support element to the agreements).

It not only became OK to ask for help (previously a taboo subject), but people were now expected to reach out for assistance. Going it alone became a part of the organization's history. Providing and asking for support even became included in the profile of the ideal leader for the business, a key element in creating a new future.

This "Applying One Lever" approach guided decisions and actions for this organization, with far-reaching implications. The expanded use of the paradoxical change approach underlying the Pay Attention to Continuity lever was evidence that the lever had been applied well.

The business succeeded with its operational objectives. Equally important, people learned how to think in a new way. They came to appreciate the power of the And paradigm in dealing with ongoing issues. Accountability alone was no solution for the CEO. It never could be. Pay attention to both poles, regardless of polarity, and find your way to a faster, easier way to a better future.

STORY: PROJECT TO SET CITYWIDE STANDARDS FOR STAY-AT-HOME CARE FOR ONE MILLION CHILDREN

Huge discrepancies existed in services offered by providers of child care in a large metropolitan area. No common standards existed. Zero shared protocols were in place. No groups had even agreed on goals against which regulations could be measured. Religious organizations, neighborhood associations, and for-profit businesses were all involved.

Some providers were members of a national group that shared best practices, held annual conferences, and had strict expectations for members. A group of local caregivers had been in operation for years and was widely recognized as providing excellent care by many parents in their part of the city. The city's health and human services department was an active player in the project, as well as parents, school officials, the city's office of management and budget, and other affected agencies.

We began our work developing common goals. Once we gained agreement on goals, we had each of the representative providers propose expectations based on their own practices. The neighborhood associations' approach of having older children mentor younger ones was considered an innovation by members of the national association. Expectations taken as matter-of-fact assumptions by the national association were news to a number of the religious organization providers.

The important lesson was to continue doing what had worked for some while also including best practices that were new for others. Continuity and change are seen once again as partners, this time in improving the children's care, instead of providers dedicating themselves to Or debates that in the end would have served no one well.

HOW TO KNOW YOU'VE APPLIED THIS LEVER WELL

❏ Previous "resisters" and "troublemakers" are celebrated as valuable contributors.

❏ Other polarities in the organization are identified and leveraged.

❏ People don't feel that they've been overrun or railroaded into change.

❏ You can point to best past and present practices that are thriving in the future.

> ❑ **Whenever change is talked about, so is continuity.**

2

THINK AND ACT AS IF THE FUTURE WERE NOW!

Start by assuming that your proposed changes are good ideas. You'd like to see them made. They'll help the organization, its customers, other external stakeholders, and employees. So why does it take so long to make these changes happen? I heard in one organization, "Even if the changes we're making are smart, by the time we get around to implementing them, they'll no longer matter." Organizations devote substantial resources to planning. But the "binder on a shelf" scenario plays out far too often. Great plans gather dust while the organization waits on its future. Here's your ticket out of the long line waiting for change implementation. Welcome to the world of Think and Act as If the Future Were Now!

A Common Problem: Change Takes Too Long

What you're trying to change in your organization makes sense. I say "trying" because there is often a gulf between the planning of change and its effective implementation. Those responsible for implementing aren't always even involved in the planning. The price for this problem is steep:

- Unclear roles
- Poor allocation of resources
- Dropped handoffs
- People inadvertently working at cross-purposes
- Indifferent effort

These are all heavy costs when change doesn't get implemented well. Working on one or more of these problems is a low-leverage place to look for making a profound improvement in the implementation game.

I believe that the main reason implementation suffers in most organizations can be found in a flawed mindset, a fundamental misconception of the way we believe the world has to work. Adopt a new paradigm. Look through a different lens, and reality itself changes. We have learned that at the quantum level, we are not passive observers of the reality we see. We live in a participatory universe.[6] We affect the world around us by what we pay attention to. If I believe the future is "out there," then that is how I experience it. It's something that will occur at some later point in time. Depending on how far out we decide it is, that's how far out we have to wait to begin experiencing it.

Solution: Think and Act as If the Future Were Now!

Make a different choice, a better one for you and your organization. Deploy the lever Think and Act as If the Future Were Now! Don't separate the future from the present. Think and act as if it were happening today. Make the line between the present and the future blurry on purpose. Stanley Davis, author of the book *Future Perfect,* counseled leaders to manage in the future perfect tense of the verb.[7] That means living the future *now* that you hope to experience later. Rather than waiting for the future you'll get to someday, choose to experience it now. Today. Immediately. Let's say you want a closer relationship with your customer. If so, stop what you're doing—right now. Look at the next interaction you have planned with this customer. If you don't have one, that might be part of your problem. How can you connect with them in a meaningful way? Should it start with a phone call, a trip to their location, or maybe a thoughtful note? Develop a plan. Implement it immediately. Put this book down. Do this other work before you read another word. Don't get to that stronger relationship someday. Begin creating it now. Live your future, today!

STORY

The executive team of a food service products company was meeting. Their goal was to draft a strategy to gain share in a new market. The conversation had been heated. The head of sales had one idea. The CEO another. The COO yet a third. All had solid reasoning behind their proposals. How to break the tie? Bring in more data. The company had been run on hunches for too long. The senior team had made a commitment to move to a more fact-based culture. The problem was that the team didn't have enough facts.

My mentor Kathie Dannemiller once said to me that when the decision isn't clear, you don't have enough information for the answer to become clear. We asked the team who could shine more light on the subject. Their answer? Salespeople in that new market. They were closest to the customer, understood the competition, and knew the company's core competencies and existing product lines. We decided to take a break and apply the lever Think and Act as If the Future Were Now! Instead of waiting for the data to be gathered at some point, the team decided to get it immediately.

Salespeople from the new market joined the meeting after the break. Those in the office did so in person; those on the road were located and did so remotely. The entire group, including the salespeople, weighed the pluses and minuses of each option against facts from the field. When push came to shove, the local sales reps unanimously endorsed the COO's recommended plan.

The decision was made based on additional facts brought to the table and engaging the salespeople in the debate in real time. Another win for the emerging culture. The most efficient communication channel in the organization (previously called the rumor mill) took care of the rest. Reports of the meeting and how it was handled were known company-wide in a day. The future wasn't something that was going to maybe, someday arrive at the organization's doorstep. It was alive and well in that conference room that very day—and within twenty-four hours had been broadcast around the world.

People who heard the story were intrigued with the idea of the salespeople being pulled into the meeting immediately after it was acknowledged that they could help in the planning. This idea took hold in different parts of the company. People started calling it "immediate change." This lever was applied during a strategic planning meeting, not as part of a formal change effort. It's a good example of what Applying One Lever looks like. Great ideas can spread naturally through an organization, paying ongoing benefits. Think of the levers as a set of these great ideas.

That's what Think and Act as If the Future Were Now! looks like. Here's a simple and powerful way to ensure that you benefit from this lever: in small ways and large, move what would typically happen later in a change process to occur earlier. If you profess to wanting greater collaboration in your organization, find ways to engage more people in working together on the task at hand. Not next month, week, or even day. Start engaging those people now. Gain the positive impact immediately.

How This Lever Helps Create Faster, Easier, Better Results

This lever is the antidote to waiting too long for change to take hold in your organization. There's no need to wait to start taking winnings off the table from the change bets you've made. You can achieve faster, easier, better results in your change work with this lever for the following five reasons:

1. *Think and Act as If the Future Were Now! demands that you get clear about your preferred future.* Encouraging people to begin immediately to make their future real means that you need to have a clear and shared picture of that future. You don't have to have every detail mapped out and know every implication in order to begin living it now. If you focus on getting your entire future right, you'll get this lever wrong. This lever is about improving every day in every way. This lever puts healthy pressure on your getting clear. A clear future can be compelling and energizing for an organization. Do yourself and others a favor. Get clear. Now.

2. *Accelerate the pace of change with Think and Act as If the Future Were Now!* Really big

changes in structures, processes, and systems take time. You'll get no disagreement from me on that score. At the same time, there's no need to wait for your post-change future to come by, pick you up, and carry you forward. Know what you want to be different, paint that picture, and then step into it. The future becomes something you create instead of something that happens to you. Be less tolerant of pushing things off for another day. This lever asks, "What can you do today to make any aspect of your desired changes real?" Free people in their daily work to begin taking action immediately. Let go of the grand rollout of better ways of doing business. Give up some of that fanfare. Make every day change day.

3. *Proof of progress is immediate.* Most change work suffers from a low "believability index." There's good reason that people step back and wait, with a "show me" attitude. This lever is the remedy to that form of resistance. Apply it, and evidence of change is all around. When people look left and right, something different and better is happening. When you're invited to join a team you were excluded from previously, it's proof that change is afoot. When a

colleague with a good idea gets new funding and people to make something happen, it's hard to deny that new and better ways are taking hold. These are not signs of earth-shattering transformation. Don't discount them either. Many immediate, small changes add up. They are your best argument to counter the show-me crowd. Make something better today, and your change effort will live to make more improvements tomorrow.

4. *You'll benefit from continuous improvements made through rapid prototyping.* This lever involves creating a rough-cut version of the change you desire. Then you test it and get feedback. Quickly revise and improve it. Test it again, gather more feedback, and repeat the cycle until you're satisfied with your results. In the world of change, this means that you're continuously introducing better and better ways to do business ... all the time. You won't have everything figured out. You and others will do that along the way. Listen to the input, improve your prototype, and try again. The whole time you're trying to improve the change, you're gaining benefits from your attempts. See how fast you can create the next prototype. Many small steps are what we

are after. It's not about big changes that take a long time to develop and implement. Instead, it's the opposite. Implement rapid prototyping and bank your benefits the whole time.

5. *You'll create an ever-larger team of changemakers.* Every person providing you feedback on your efforts gets a jersey. They're now a member of your team. They become invested in what is now your shared success. They'll want to see what's changed in your next prototype based on their feedback. Was it helpful? Did you use it? You're creating an automatic PR machine. The larger your team, the more momentum you build. The team continues to expand as existing members invite their friends and colleagues to aid in the cause. The energy you used to put into communication campaigns and creating cases for change? Redirect it to getting change work done better and better.

STORY

I once had a social services agency client in charge of providing day care for stay-at-home parents. It had just increased its contributions by 8 percent in a down economic environment and had finally broken the $100,000 ceiling on donations. There was much to celebrate at the end-of-year board meeting—until the board chair shared an insight. She said, "There are two thousand children that we serve every year. It costs $4,000 per year to provide care for them. And we have to do it for five years, until they begin school. Do the math. We have a $40 million problem on our hands, and we're celebrating breaking the $100,000 mark." The board chair had pointed out a sobering truth. The agency was woefully falling short of its ultimate goal. It was time to innovate. Big-time.

What would be an entirely new path into the future for this organization? Incremental change wouldn't do. The leadership had to up their game significantly if they were serious about making a difference in the real problem. They needed to start thinking and acting as if they had a $40 million problem. It changed everything about how they approached their work. Because board members had a much larger problem to solve, they found a seat at tables with people with deeper pockets. They took on mentors from larger nonprofits, who taught them how to do business as if they were already the more substantial entity they wanted to be.

They were living their future today. The organization became more capable as a result of using the Think and Act as If the Future Were Now! lever. Its improvement year over year was remarkable. Although it didn't match that $40 million goal, it increased its revenue stream by 600 percent the following year. This lever accelerates changes of all types, moving you further, faster into your preferred future.

Success Factors in Applying This Lever

What are the keys to making your future happen faster? Ensure that you have the following factors in place. They are your guide to changing your mindset and your methods.

Factor One: Embrace This New Paradigm

None of this works if you don't believe it will. People can tell when you're only partially invested or doubting what you're asking them to believe. You need to be the one leading the charge to see and be different in the world.

Once you start thinking this way, you'll never not do it again. You'll find yourself walking the halls of your organization, sitting in meetings, or having casual conversations and see opportunities to Think and Act as if the Future Were Now! Maybe you already approach change this way. If so, you'll have an easy job of it. If, by contrast, your own "believability index" is low and this seems like a bunch of hooey, play along for a day, week, or month. Stretch your timeline as you prove to yourself the value of this new worldview. Change doesn't have to take ages. You and others can create it, right now.

Factor Two: Envision a Winning Future

This lever makes the future happen faster. Therefore, it's essential to have the future you are envisioning be a successful one for your organization. Make sure it's one that you want. You'll be experiencing it faster than you believed possible. With the wrong future, you run the risk of rapidly and effectively failing. You don't want to go down a path of wasted time, money, energy, and other resources. Create a future that people want to call their own, and you're on a near-certain positive path. Having a picture of success in mind will help you take full advantage of this lever.

Factor Three: Get More People Asking the Question, "If We Were in Our Preferred Future, How Would We Approach This Situation?"

It's a simple question with profound consequences. The greater the number of people in your organization asking this question, the faster you'll create your future. Asking the question guides people into a future-focused mindset. The more that people talk about this question, the clearer their picture of the future becomes. It's not about gaining immediate agreement. It's the conversation that matters. Exploring this question is like breathing life into your future. The best way to test for alignment is through these conversations. Would we take the same action? Do we have different assumptions? Answering these questions prevents problems from occurring. Celebrate similarities in responses. Pay attention to differences. Keep this conversation alive and well in your organization.

Factor Four: Fail Fast, Learn, and Improve

Wasn't failure supposed to be a bad thing, something to avoid? That's true with a flawed future; you're aiming to achieve the wrong results. This success factor of failing fast, learning, and making course corrections has to do with how you're changing, not where you're heading. Don't avoid trying new approaches out of a fear of failure. Organizations that fail the fastest—and learn from these shortfalls—have a distinct advantage when it comes to change. If people are tiptoeing around, afraid to be the first one to screw up, you'll never be able to apply this lever. Risk-averse organizations take special note: it needs to be OK to make mistakes.

Factor Five: Communicate Lessons Learned, Far and Wide

Learning doesn't count if you're the only one taking the lessons to heart. Unshared learning leads to repeated mistakes. Working your change effort on many fronts at once will lead to a whole lot of learning. With fast cycle times, improvement ideas will come in bunches, not one at a time. Don't count on osmosis for lessons to be shared. Once you know a better way forward, you're responsible for sharing it with others. Be open to what someone else learned that's better than what you did. Look for the best of the best. Don't sit on your successes. Every attempt you make at changing is on behalf of the entire organization. Be accountable for sharing insights and aha moments. Dead ends are equally important for people to know about.

STORY

We were once coaching a senior executive experiencing conflict with a direct report who was a valuable member of the team and who had special expertise needed by the group to be successful. Despite her best efforts, the executive had been unable to break through in this particular relationship. The whole team was suffering. The senior executive had heard from others that this disconnect was beginning to be a problem for internal customers, not just for members of her team. Applying this lever, we decided to take a different course of action—and now.

In the midst of a regular coaching session, the senior executive asked her direct report to come join the meeting. If they were going to have to work together better in the future, they might as well begin working together better now. Although apprehensive, the executive's direct report joined our meeting. We explained the situation and our goal of advancing this agenda in real time in the meeting, right then and there. We then described the idea behind the Think and Act as If the Future Were Now! lever and how it worked.

The executive began by asking the direct report to describe his ideal future. What would it look, feel, and sound like going forward if things were working well for all? To both of their surprises, they had similar images of success. The key to this lever is not waiting for another time to make a change. Improve the situation right here and now for maximum impact.

What would be different the rest of that day to make this newly discovered shared vision real? What new assumptions and behaviors could they try out ... that afternoon? No grand plans and big commitments, just a little rapid prototyping. Once they mapped out the rest of the day, we took that as enough of a test case to get started. The next morning, we all compared notes. What had worked and could be built on? What problems still remained? Each subsequent test of the lever went for a bit longer, until full weeks were being planned and implemented at a time.

Short cycle times and immediate improvements are key ingredients to getting the best out of this lever. You won't get the future right the first time, every time. Be comfortable with close misses and larger gaffes alike. These are new behaviors. The important part is to get started living your future now. Do that, and you'll begin experiencing it sooner.

How to Know You've Applied This Lever Well

Grade yourself against the items discussed in the next sections. Each serves as a proof point in evaluating how well you've changed the paradigm and practices in your organization to take full advantage of this lever.

The Speed of Change Accelerates Dramatically

Your future happens faster when you adopt this lever. You'll know you've done it well when you're surprised by the pace of change. In the past, you may have gotten used to falling behind on timelines and milestones. Now, you'll be ahead of the game. I've often told leaders who were frustrated with the prior pace of change in their organization to prepare for a new reality and that they'll more often than not become the bottleneck for positive and productive change. They need to get ready for increased expectations from their people. Not just to "walk the talk" but to "run the talk" a bit. People want new skills and knowledge. Learning and development departments benefit from an upsurge in requests. Collaboration becomes more than an aspiration or value on a piece of paper. Requests for cross-functional teams and meetings increase as well—and now. Informal communication across business units and functional teams becomes the norm.

You Experience Change More Than You Talk about It

Change becomes less of a topic for conversation and more an action in the real world. Instead of hearing unending dialogues that lead nowhere, you witness new behaviors. The organization begins operating in ways that make sense. Decisions get made and actions taken in shorter cycle times. Approvals no longer require people to wait weeks; they're agreed on in days. Better yet, how about sign-offs in real time when possible? People are asking the question, "How would we be doing this if we were in our preferred future today?" If there's more studying and careful consideration needed as part of your future decision-making, it still gets done, just faster. The time lag between planning and implementation goes away. Change becomes a verb that is acted on more than a noun that gets discussed.

Cynicism Decreases as Evidence Increases

Often people are cynical about change. But when you use the Think and Act as if the Future Were Now! lever, the evidence of change is all around you. And with that evidence comes optimism, hope for a better today and tomorrow. People look for possibilities and become part of a virtuous cycle. They see things get better and then experience that "better" for themselves. Leaders listen. People who used to be humored have influence. The usual "This too shall pass" mantra gives way to a new call for action and proof that business is being done in new ways. Do all the right choices get made all the time?

No. Are changes taking hold, being tested, and improved over time? Yes. Suspicion about needed changes gives way to momentum for them.

The Line between Planning and Implementation Blurs

People typically draw a line between planning and implementation. First, we plan. Then we implement. The line exists only because we create it. Give up that make-believe distinction. When you blur the line between the two, you can plan while you implement and implement while you plan. Planning gives you a rough road map with which to begin your journey. Implementation gives you the opportunity to test assumptions and make real-time course corrections. We manufactured the line between planning and implementation in the first place. We have the power to erase it. No need to argue about which you're doing when. Do them both together, and Think and Act as if the Future Were Now!

Energy Increases in the Organization

People get excited when they see their future happening faster. They can't help it. This excitement builds on itself over time. When I see you making a change I've dreamed of for some time, it stokes my fire. Now, channel this energy toward a common future. After many failed attempts in the past, it may take people a while to believe it's true. There's often a delayed reaction as people wait for things to snap back to the same old, same old. When the future is happening all around you, it's increasingly hard to deny. With these shifts, that latent resource that resides in all organizations becomes available. Call it discretionary effort. Extra motivation. The organization's limitless resource of its people's energy. You'll know it when you see it. Your organization will become a force to be reckoned with.

Examples of This Lever in Action

Stopping a pending pandemic of tuberculosis in a large city and finding common ground among thirty-two stakeholder groups agreeing on pollution control measures—these are both complex efforts with the health and well-being of millions of people in the balance. Accelerating the pace of change was a win in each story. Read on and see how it happened.

STORY: COLLABORATION BETWEEN DEPARTMENTS IN A LARGE US CITY

A large US city was on the front lines of a tuberculosis outbreak threatening to become a pandemic. If the disease could be contained in the city, it could be contained in the world. The goal was to create a TB blueprint for the entire city. Five city agencies needed to partner together in ways they never had before. They had to agree on common protocols, develop joint budgets, negotiate roles, and ensure successful handoffs of patients between hospitals, homeless shelters, and, in some cases, even the prison system. A large, complex network of collaboration needed to be created—in short order.

A large group meeting was held, attended by representatives from each agency. Four hundred people in all. A subgroup was charged during the meeting with devising common treatment protocols. Word got back to our consulting team that the subgroup had all but devolved into constant debate. There was no listening or negotiating, and no people budging a bit on their positions. Everyone wanted their protocols to be adopted by the other agencies. The required collaboration was far from the reality in the room.

We stuck our heads in the breakout room and said we had heard they were having some trouble. A few members of the group begrudgingly admitted as much. We asked if they wanted help sorting through their issues. Again, subtle agreement registered around the room. After we were sitting in the group for a few minutes, one of the problems became obvious. Two of the people in the room were leading a raucous argument, listening to nobody and dominating the floor time.

After giving two warnings, we asked the two to leave the room and return when they had settled their differences. They both stormed out. The rest of the group kept working. About twenty minutes later, the two returned. They said that they realized that their organizations were going to have to listen to each other back in the real world, so they might as well try doing it themselves during this meeting. They made a proposal. It wasn't a perfect solution, but it started the conversation in helpful ways toward an agreement that everyone could support.

The collaboration needed for the solution to have a lasting impact had been witnessed in the room in real time. The two who had gotten in the way of others invited the rest of the group to begin living the collaborative future they had discovered. The TB story had a positive outcome as the epidemic was beaten back through never-before-experienced levels of cooperation among the agencies.

The Think and Act as If the Future Were Now! lever was instrumental in this story, as the needed collaboration had to be brought into the room that afternoon. Without that, the group would at best be making only surface-level agreements. Instead they had an experience of the kind of collaboration that was going to be needed in the future. They began living it in real time. People needed to bring their future into the meeting room. They did, and the world has them to thank for it.

STORY: ALIGNING THIRTY-TWO STAKEHOLDERS AROUND AN AIR QUALITY INITIATIVE

A broad-based group of thirty-two stakeholder organizations gathered together to kick off a two-year project to improve pollution in the Pacific Northwest of the United States. Federal and state government; local agencies; Native American tribes; academics; non-governmental organizations; and agricultural, business, industrial, health, and public interest organizations were all represented. Each had its own point of view on the problem and its own beliefs about what would be the best solutions. Unfortunately, and predictably, these solutions were not the same. Some were aligned. Others conflicted.

The large team of two hundred people working together on the project needed to establish a baseline understanding of the history of pollution in the region, its health and ecosystem effects, and the existing regulatory programs and initiatives. Each stakeholder group was charged with educating the rest of the project members on their organization's work on the issue and its proposed solutions. Everybody had to make their assumptions and proposed plans visible so that conflicts could be easily seen and necessary solutions identified. Representatives from all stakeholder groups created a comprehensive plan.

There were complicated negotiations involving every stakeholder. More people were invited into the substantive work of the project. Without them, we might still be negotiating between entrenched groups rooted in old assumptions, with no new perspectives from outsiders. The more your present can look like your future, the better shot you have at finding solutions that work for all.

Leaders from each stakeholder group partnered to create a draft plan to address these contentious issues. Then they thought and acted as if the future were now. The draft plan was presented to all two hundred delegates with a request that they improve it. The large group offered their best thinking to the leadership team. Instead of "taking it under advisement," the leaders went to work immediately reviewing and integrating the recommendations. Overnight, they, and a subset of other delegates, turned around the new version of the plan. No waiting until next quarter, month, or week to unveil the road map forward. It was done the next day.

Seventeen "promising projects" were launched immediately. Stakeholders partnered to move these efforts forward in ways they couldn't have imagined just days earlier. Positive and productive relationships were created in real time during the overnight working session. This progress was advanced further the following day. Both leaders and other meeting attendees accelerated the trust, collaboration, and agreements to improve air quality in the Pacific Northwest.

HOW TO KNOW YOU'VE APPLIED THIS LEVER WELL

❑ The speed of change accelerates dramatically.

❑ You experience change more than you talk about it.

❑ Cynicism decreases as evidence increases.

❑ The line between planning and implementation blurs.

❑ Energy increases in the organization.

3

DESIGN IT YOURSELF

The Design It Yourself lever is an invitation for creativity. It gives you the opportunity and responsibility to develop change efforts, processes, and tools that fit for you and your organization. You're also encouraged to revise them as needed as you move forward in your work. Many ten-step formulas, eight-phase methods, and six-point prescriptions exist to guide you through change efforts. Don't feel trapped following someone else's recipe for success. At the same time, don't ignore them. Adopt and adapt what works for you. Toss the rest. Do only the work you need to ensure success.

A Common Problem: People Reject Your Change Approach Because It's "Not Invented Here"

The Not Invented Here (NIH) chorus is a major problem experienced by leaders and change agents in organizations of all types. This ailment slows many change efforts before they even get out of the starting gate. There's a saying, "We own what we help create." The corollary is equally true: "We resist what is forced on us by others." Begin a change effort, and the questions come faster than you can answer them. Have you tried this in our industry? What about with a company of our size? Do you have experience helping organizations with [insert kind of change needed]?

The NIH call is a surefire ingredient for frustration and debates. When you're stuck arguing about the merits of an approach, you're no longer using it to advantage. Time, energy, money, and political capital get wasted instead of being invested as you navigate your way forward. The beginning of change work is the point of greatest opportunity. That's when you decide who gets involved, how, and when. Everything afterward is implementation of these original plans. When stuck with using a fixed approach (read: someone else's), you lose degrees of freedom when they mean the most.

Solution: Design It Yourself

The Design It Yourself lever takes this resistance off the table, immediately and completely. No one can complain that the organization has directly imported someone else's answer to their problem, whether it's a fine fit or not. This lever doesn't preclude you from using best practices. It warns you against adopting approaches without considering how suitable they are to your organization's culture, strengths, and weaknesses. You need to define the unique purpose, outcomes, and road map for your change work. Even when actual changes are predetermined, the more control that people in an organization have over how those changes will be made, the less resistance you will encounter. Approaches defined by the people responsible for making changes are easily adopted by the individual, team, or organization doing the changing. This lever does a great job of addressing the typical resistance of NIH straight away.

STORY

This lever added great value when we were working with a publishing company responsible for production and distribution of six regional newspapers. The Design It Yourself lever made sense to this organization—the design of its papers was a differentiator for it in the marketplace. The purpose of the effort was to solidify success into the future with a stronger, more aligned team.

There was no grand plan when we began this work. The organization had been successfully in business for thirty years, but still did not have a documented vision and values to point the way forward. The founders sketched these out and introduced them to the rest of the staff with a warm invitation to improve them. Editing was a core competence of the operation, so there already existed a culture of improving drafts. Members of the production, sales, and editorial staffs all added their best thinking—the vast majority of these suggestions were integrated into the final document.

The head of sales asked whether we were going to do any work with people separately, as he emphasized individual sales goals with his team. We used an approach developed by Peter Block called Your Vision of Greatness.[8] Each staff member created a videotaped talk about what their work and the company's work would look like when the vision and values were alive and well. People asked questions, and challenged and affirmed each other. Staff members reported never feeling as empowered as they did during this activity.

Handoffs of work within and between departments had been a problem as far back as anyone could remember. Well-intentioned people dropped balls, making work harder for others. We mapped all core processes in the organization, redesigned those that needed it, and improved both performance and personal relationships among staff.

Some coaching for the newly created leadership team, comprising all department heads and the founders, rounded out this project. With this client, we figured out the next step in the process based on successfully completing the previous one, all while having the organization design its own change effort. We followed the client's lead, responding to requests and suggestions that made sense for the publisher based on past practices, need, and the vision and values.

How This Lever Helps Create Faster, Easier, Better Results

This lever transforms NIH resistance into commitment to your cause. You don't have to force-fit someone else's approach to your unique organization. You can achieve faster, easier, better results in your change work by using this lever for the following five reasons:

1. *You gain immediate and lasting ownership of the work ahead.* Instead of butting up against resistance because your approach wasn't homegrown, you'll find pride and a commitment to ensuring that self-made plans succeed. If things go awry at any point, there's no finger-pointing. Co-creating the path forward leads people to be much more willing to forgive the inevitable mistakes and missteps that lie ahead.

2. *Your approach fits your needs.* Unique organizations deserve unique approaches. Your organization's experiences with prior change efforts and its current capabilities regarding change should be accounted for in your approach. People will be more receptive to your efforts if they fit your organization's culture. If a certain group needs to be involved early, involve them early. If two functions have to work through particular issues, bring them together to work on the issues. No two change efforts need ever be the same.

3. *What needs to be achieved in your effort gets achieved.* You define the purpose of your effort and its outcomes based on current realities. You amend them as needed as

you proceed. The right change work gets done the right way for your organization. Ultimately this leads to the right changes being made faster, easier, and better than if you tried to force-fit a predetermined approach onto your business. You're more likely to win the game of change when you're the one making the rules.

4. *People better understand the approach being used because they created it.* This understanding translates to work being done the way it's supposed to be, based on a common, agreed-on plan where there is deep ownership and insight. Better understanding of the work you're doing, and why you're doing it, translates into greater confidence in the plans you've developed. People throughout your organization understand their contributions to the cause and are therefore better able to deliver on their parts of the process.

5. *People learn how change is best made in their organization.* Lessons you learn today about creating better ways of working will benefit you tomorrow. Knowing which change approaches work and which don't in your organization is valuable information. You will avoid making the same mistakes twice when you design your own change efforts.

People are smarter about how, when, and whether course corrections are needed in your current effort. When you design your own change work, you'll also be more capable of making needed revisions to it in the future.

Success Factors in Applying This Lever

The next sections describe seven factors for getting the best from this lever. Work your way through them, setting yourself up for success in the near and far terms. When you use Design It Yourself, you need the right people, good data, clear goals, and a solid plan. Read on to learn how to ensure success when you're blazing your own trail.

Factor One: Get the Right People Involved from the Start

It's better not to engage the organization at all than for leaders to begin with false promises about the influence people will have and then pull the rug out from under them partway through their work. Set initial boundaries about what is fair game and what's off-limits. Much time typically gets spent considering leaders' expectations of the organization. It's equally important for the organization's expectations of senior executives to be clarified. Consider the knowledge, skills, and abilities people will require to provide the leadership needed for the effort to succeed. In some cases, these may already be in place. In others, they'll need to be developed or to be brought into the organization. Next, think about the best people to serve on a design team. This group of people responsible for guiding your change work is a microcosm of the organization. Bring cynics, zealots, and everyone in between to the team. We've had teams as small as eight and as large as forty. Ensuring diversity of thought is critical. There is no magic number.

Factor Two: Learn from Your Organization's Past Experiences with Change

Approaches used in past change efforts should inform your present one. When you study past practices, you'll gain valuable insights that will help you create faster, easier, better results this time around. Invite some who were directly involved in these past efforts to join your design team. Have them tell stories. Distill the lessons they learned. Secrets for addressing today's challenges can be found in yesterday's successes and failures. Take the time needed to understand not only what happened but also why. Look for clues beyond the obvious. Don't be satisfied with a cursory look back.

Factor Three: Get Your Arms around as Much of the Mess as You Can

There's a common saying that leads to misguided decisions early in change efforts: "Let's cut this problem down to size." It's the same as thinking that if we could only simplify the situation enough, we could succeed! The Design It Yourself lever is about dealing with all of the messy reality you find yourself facing, not just what fits into the original scope of your project definition. Leave as few stones unturned as possible when searching for clues about where the best moves lie in designing your change effort. Opening the floodgates of reality can be overwhelming. We think our odds of success go up when we understand our circumstances. Lean into the confusion. Comfort will not serve you well. Take a step back. See the patterns underlying the obvious. Remember that what we're after is doing the right work more easily, not the easy work right.

An oft-repeated concern among change leaders is "scope creep." I encourage clients to look for opportunities to extend the work beyond the original boundaries set, when that's needed. Focus on the work that needs to be done—not merely the work you originally decided to do. Define and redefine the scope of your change effort based on what you learn as you progress. Ensure that the lines you draw make sense based on reality as you now know it. Defying the so-called common wisdom of scope creep may be the best way to get where you need to go.

Factor Four: Creatively Expand What You Think You Know

Once I blindfolded an executive team and had them board a bus, not knowing where they were going. While complaining about not being able to see the road ahead, one leader said something that stopped the grumbling in its tracks: "I bet this is how our people end up feeling most of the time. Blindfolded and not being able to see the strategy or our future." The impact of this statement guided our work for months to come. We took the blindfolds off at the end of the bus trip of leaders from this packaged foods producer after arriving at an innovative grocery store that stocked their goods. Our purpose? To learn what led the grocer to hold a significant competitive advantage in the marketplace. What set it apart? Some answers we learned on the trip in addition to the insight about the lack of a shared strategy throughout the operation: who ever heard of a grocery store day care? What about a food court where the community held weddings? These leaders came up with innovative approaches to expanding their markets. Out-of-the-box thinking leads to out-of-the-box solutions.

In another case, we were struggling with how to explain scenario planning to a design team of drivers, mechanics, and route planners. A member had a light bulb go off. He said, "It's like Mr. Potato Head. You can change the eyes, nose, and legs. It's just a different version of the original toy." We later held Mr. and Mrs. Potato Head strategy sessions to help everyone in the organization understand the complexity of addressing the various combinations of whom they would serve, where, and how. Get smart about the world you're living and working in—any and every way you can.

Factor Five: Define a Clear Purpose and Outcomes

Answering the question of why you're engaging in a change effort is not as simple as saying "to beat the competition." In his landmark book *The Practice of Management,* Peter Drucker championed the importance of an organization being crystal clear about its mission, or the business it was in.[9] Not what it does, but *why* it does what it does. The same can be said about a change effort. There are four criteria you can use to test whether you have a solid purpose statement to guide your change effort:

1. *Is results oriented, not activity based.* Use an old quality tool called the "5 Whys Analysis." You start by asking why you're undertaking this effort, and keep asking why you're taking the prior action until you arrive at the underlying result you need to accomplish.

2. *Speaks to all stakeholders.* Test the purpose with different stakeholders in your change effort to make sure they understand and are energized by it.

3. *Responds to your challenges and opportunities.* Compare the purpose to your current

realities. It should be unique and directly related to the issues you are facing.

4. *Is ennobling.* Check whether the purpose would call forth your greater selves and better angels. You need to be proud to be associated with the work you'll be doing in line with this statement. My mentor Kathie Dannemiller believed in this criteria deeply.

Outcomes for your change effort should define the metrics by which you'll measure success. They are the high-level deliverables that are nonnegotiable. Without them clearly spelled out, you'll never even know when your work is done.

Factor Six: Develop a Road Map That Will Achieve Your Purpose and Outcomes

Your next task is to answer a series of questions that will allow you to map out the work ahead. There may be models, approaches, and processes that you've used in the past that will serve you well now. Designing it yourself doesn't mean you need to start from scratch. It also doesn't mean that you can't. There are dozens of different ways to do that. For example:

• Use past practices that worked

- Explore innovative ideas you've never tried before
- Decide to convene large groups of several hundred or small groups of work teams
- Meet face-to-face or organize yourselves virtually
- Choose to include hard numbers and people's feelings
- Analyze facts and ask questions

Design It Yourself means making these decisions so that you achieve your purpose and outcomes.

Factor Seven: Check Your Plans and Change Them as Needed

Design It Yourself means that you'll be traveling terrain not navigated before. Do some quality control. Will the planned activities and events help you achieve your purpose and outcomes? Are your purpose and outcomes responsive to what you've learned in your study of what's happening inside and outside your organization?

Testing should occur throughout the life of your change effort.

- Have we made the progress we anticipated?
- Are we ahead of schedule or behind? Why or why not?

- Is what we're asking of people realistic and achievable?
- Will the support we need from people lead to there being too much on their plates?

These questions need to focus on learning. Leave your defensiveness at the door. When someone raises an issue, remember the four magic words: "Can you say more?" The more informed you are, the faster and better you'll be able to create change.

STORY

A client of mine was caught in what they called a death spiral. This energy company's business unit was delivering poor performance, and had been for quite a while. The worse its performance, the less investment it received from corporate to dig itself out of its hole. The less investment it received, the less competitive it was able to be. And that led to poorer performance ... and around and around it went. This vicious cycle had a choke hold on the organization.

Senior leaders had already committed to becoming a model of high involvement in every facet of the business. We talked with the design team about the need to get the right people in the room to gain this needed alignment. It would be important for both formal and informal leaders to be clear about what they were getting into and what would be expected of them to make this change effort successful. I still remember, it was over the 4th of July weekend when we asked the design team to think about who these people might be.

When we returned after the holiday, the design team members tossed a stapled stack of papers across the table. We had expected twenty, maybe thirty people to be identified. There were three hundred names on the list. In a business unit of twelve hundred employees. We tried to explain to the team what we meant by formal and informal leadership. Maybe they had misunderstood us. In response, they said, "You told us to compile a list of those people required to lead this change effort if it is to be successful. Those are the people." It was a wake-up call for our consulting team and time to redesign in real time.

At first it seemed odd that one-fourth of the entire organization was defined as leaders. It was a different path than the one we'd originally imagined. At some level, everyone in an organization has a leadership role to play. The difference here was that what we expected to be a group of at most thirty to lead out on this effort was in fact much larger.

In this same organization, we later held a three-day meeting of a thousand people. This large group meeting was attended by 85 percent of the members of the business unit. They left only skeletal crews on the platforms—enough so that they did not need to shut down operations. This larger group reached consensus on ten actions to save their business. And save the business they did. Eventually they made it back into the good graces of corporate and got funding for the required new technologies.

Including such a large proportion of the organization in a single event is a seemingly radical move—unless your leaders have committed to creating a high-involvement culture. Nearly everyone in the organization decided on the changes they needed to make. It was the right call for this business. It provided a very visible way for senior leaders to show the rest of the organization that they were serious about involvement. Your takeaway: identify the right changes to be made with the right people the right way—for your organization.

How to Know You've Applied This Lever Well

You've created your own change effort, but how do you know you've done it well? Review the elements discussed here and mark yourself against the checklist at the end of the chapter. If you've done a decent but not great job, return to the drawing board. Refine your purpose and outcomes. Revisit your road map. Make sure you have a good agenda for the work that lies ahead.

You Have a Shared Picture of Your Organization's Past and Present

As you apply this lever, you may have a hard time finding quick consensus. Don't worry. The goal is a shared picture, not the same picture. People's perspectives are shaped by where they call home in the organization. Different places lead to different points of view. My mentor Kathie Dannemiller was fond of saying, "Each person's truth is truth." Don't assume you know another's story. The more complete your picture, the more accurate it becomes. Listen for the darker stories in the organization as well as the lighter ones. For some, difficult times might be harder to discuss. For others, celebrating success might be challenging. Do you understand not only these stories but also the reasons underlying them? Look for the patterns that have helped shape your organization's journey.

Anyone Can Understand Your Purpose, Outcomes, and Road Map

The crucible of conversations needs to purify the words and meaning of your purpose, outcomes, and road map. Anyone in the organization, and all its external key stakeholders, should readily understand why you're undertaking your change work. Plain words are your friends in this task. The easiest way for people to join your cause is for them to immediately connect to it. It needs to speak to their hopes, desires, and dreams as well as the tough circumstances they've found themselves in. This is not about pushing your agenda through the organization. It's about engaging people in conversations that matter. Find people not already on your design team. Listen to them, consider their suggestions, and make needed changes. You can be proud of your work—just don't protect it from improvements others think are needed.

Your Road Map Will Achieve Your Purpose and Outcomes, and Your Purpose and Outcomes Respond to Your Current Realities

There are straightforward checks and balances that will also let you know whether you've applied this lever well. Just as your current realities shaped your purpose and outcomes, and your purpose and outcomes guided your activities and the sequencing of them, the same should be true in reverse. When you find a disconnect in this chain, you have more work to do. The more people who can follow this internal logic, the more likely you are of success in the long run. Find your "Joes," the fellow mentioned earlier in the book who stood in the doorway for a half day before joining the design team. If these people are confident that you're on a good path, you can trust that you likely are.

There Are Unique Elements of Your Change Effort That Fit the Distinctive Aspects of Your Organization

How can someone tell that your road map, purpose, and outcomes are specifically designed for your effort and company? What stories can you tell about why there are particular parts of your plan that are spot-on for your organization? You should be able to articulate clearly why certain people are engaged in one way and others in another. If you've got a generic approach, you'll get generic results. Take advantage of this lever to make sure you have the right plan for you. Why do you need an extra two phases for your effort when an off-the-shelf approach you're adapting has five? What are those extra steps going to get you that are critical to your success? If you don't have good reasons for what you're up to, you should be up to something different.

Examples of This Lever in Action

A global energy company and regional transit organization were faced with very different challenges. See how they designed their change efforts from purpose and outcomes through to detailed plans, each charting its own course forward based on its unique situation.

STORY: CULTURE INTEGRATION IN A GLOBAL ENERGY COMPANY

This effort was implemented in a company that, post-merger, had a presence in more than fifty-four countries and employed thirty-seven thousand people. Culture integration has been identified as a primary factor in why mergers and acquisitions fail to deliver promised results.[10] The tough challenge for all M&As is to create a well-integrated culture that retains the best aspects of each organization while leaving their respective weaknesses behind.

The Culture Integration Team—our design team for this work—developed the following purpose, outcomes, and five-phase process for the two years of work in their organization.

PURPOSE OF THE CHANGE EFFORT

To fully realize the financial and operational advantages afforded by the merger through creating a strong, unified culture that drives dramatically improved performance when compared to the legacy companies.

OUTCOMES OF THE CHANGE EFFORT

• Aligning the business strategy and needed culture

• Accelerating the cultural integration of the two companies

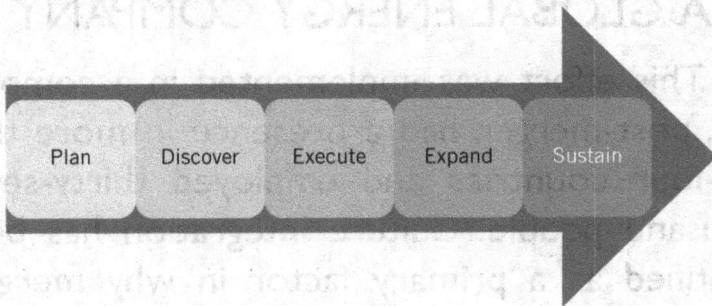

| Plan | Discover | Execute | Expand | Sustain |

The Culture Integration Road Map

• Assessing talent in both organizations to aid in the selection process along with new leader assimilation and executive coaching

• Developing integrated change management processes and the leadership skills needed to support the change in culture

Phase 1: Plan

The first phase of this effort included reaching agreements and contracting with the CEO and senior executives on the approach, parameters, requirements for success, and personal commitments needed to set the work up for success. Based on these agreements, our consulting team developed a first draft of the high-level five-phase road map depicted in the figure. This included the creation of the

Culture Integration Team (CIT), whose charge it would be to develop the purpose and outcomes and refine the five-step plan.

Phase 2: Discover

A culture assessment comprising individual and group interviews kicked off this second phase of work. Significant differences existed between the two organizations. The first company was more top down in management style, less disciplined in developing and implementing processes, and more bureaucratic than its new partner. Both companies benefited from hardworking employees and suffered from operating in silos. Safety was also a strong value in both organizations.

The CIT launched during this second phase. This design team built pictures of the two organizations' current cultures and learned about the 8 Levers. They also defined the purpose and outcomes and refined the road map for the change effort. Applying the Design It Yourself lever, they decided that the senior executives would draft a company vision, and employees would be invited to provide feedback on this first draft. The model was based on the approach described in the book *Full Steam Ahead* by Ken Blanchard and Jesse Stoner.[11] This approach defines vision as the combination of who we are (purpose), where we're headed (picture of the future), and how we're going to get there (values and behaviors).

Feedback on the vision and implementation plans would be developed through six global large group events. Five of the summits would be held in the organization's different regions, with two hundred participants attending each. The groups would be made up of a mix of people across the organization from the hosting region and the rest of the world. The CIT adopted a "consolidation" strategy for crafting the business's unified culture. The five regional summits would be followed by an action summit. At this meeting, representatives from each regional summit would consolidate their and other employees' input, translating the desired culture into daily operations.

Phase 3: Execute

Monthly CIT meetings were held to design the regional summits and manage the overall change effort. Each of the five two-day events educated participants on challenges facing the business. All participants were asked to analyze the culture assessment from phase 2 and provide feedback on the vision. People also received a short course in change and the choices they had about how to approach it—as

"Learners" or "Judgers," based on work by Marilee Adams's *Change Your Questions, Change Your Life.*[12] Preliminary organization-wide plans were developed for how the draft vision could be implemented. Personal commitments were made to bring the vision to life, including how lessons learned could be communicated to others in the company. Representative cross-section table groups also selected their delegates to attend the action summit.

Work in this phase also included the CIT's consolidating recommended improvements to the vision developed at each regional summit. Specific behaviors were identified that would be evidence that each value had been adopted by the organization. The CIT provided senior executives with a document that highlighted all changes and the number of people in each summit who had voted for various revisions. The senior team used these suggestions to create the vision in its final form.

Phase 4: Expand

This fourth phase focused on expanding the experiences and decisions beyond the thousand people who had already participated in the effort. The action summit was the first step in addressing this challenge. A few groups that had participated in the regional summits and already taken action on their commitments shared culture integration success stories with the action summit large group. Leading-edge thinking in the field of culture change was explored, key strategies for expanding the work analyzed, and high-impact change initiatives identified. Tools to support sustained culture change were introduced and plans developed to apply them back on the job.

An opportunity to redesign in real time became available through the design and facilitation of "mini regional summits" of twenty-five to one hundred people. Representatives who had attended the regional summits hosted these mini-summits as a way to connect colleagues to the larger work being done in the organization. A second emergent part of the plan involved a company-wide monthly focus on each value. Frontline work teams discussed what each value meant to them, where they'd seen it already applied in the organization, and how they could personally live the values in their daily work. Teams engaged in deep dialogues. People wrote full pages responding to these simple, yet pointed, questions. A third strategy was to hold meetings where functions made commitments to one another about better ways they would work together. All three of these "redesign in real time" opportunities were leveraged for change despite not being part of the original project plans.

Phase 5: Sustain

Work in this fifth phase focused on embedding the integrated culture in every aspect of the organization. The values and behaviors were incorporated into how projects across the entire company were managed. The desired culture drove the design of sales meetings and other already existing events. For example, the "One Team" value guided the space planning and work areas in a new office opened in one region. Frontline production workers instituted a "Culture Creator" program complete with helmet stickers for those acknowledged by their peers of living the new, integrated culture. At the one-year mark, our consulting team conducted a survey, which found that the integrated culture had taken hold in several core business processes, a new company-wide IT system, and daily work throughout the organization.

STORY: LEADERSHIP TEAM EFFECTIVENESS IN A REGIONAL TRANSIT COMPANY

This application of the Design It Yourself lever occurred at a successful public transportation business. The levers had been applied with substantial success to an organization-wide improvement effort during the previous decade. The regional provider had recently won state and national awards for performance and innovation, and had also achieved improvements in operating costs, productivity, and customer satisfaction.

However, a substantial service expansion was in the works. The senior team would be called on to provide a new level of leadership to an organization serving a much larger, more complex footprint. These executives were responsible for directing the efforts of mechanics, drivers, route planners, and shared services. There was a window of opportunity to strengthen the team's basic work processes, such as meetings, budgeting, and cross-functional collaboration. As well, a new CEO had recently taken the reins, leading to a need to adapt to his management style.

To begin, we conducted individual interviews with senior staff and board members. Insights from these interviews helped define the purpose, outcomes, and road map. Individual board members were seen by staff as having pet projects. Longtime employees knew how to do their jobs, but there was little documentation of these processes. Staff complained about daily practices, such as meetings, cross-functional planning, and prioritizing, while the board listed the most urgent work as fiscal management and board–staff relations.

Working with these findings and their own understanding of their team, senior staff developed the purpose, outcomes, and road map described here.

PURPOSE OF THE CHANGE EFFORT

To take our leadership to the next level by improving how we operate as a team and individually so that we are best positioned for success in developing and implementing our next strategic plan.

OUTCOMES OF THE CHANGE EFFORT

• Develop abilities to design and manage meetings so that we take best advantage of the limited time we have together as a team.

• Establish stronger relationships between members of the team so that we can engage in healthy dialogues, debates, and discussions.

• Ensure mutually supportive behaviors among team members, especially with the CEO.

• Understand change and how it affects us so that we are better able to lead change with our people.

ROAD MAP FOR THE CHANGE EFFORT

An adaptation of Jay Galbraith's Star Model[13] formed the foundation for the yearlong engagement at this transit company. Work streams and projects were defined and completed for each element of Galbraith's model (i.e., Strategy, Structure, Processes, Rewards, and People).

A Look inside the Change Effort

Applying the Design It Yourself lever involved customizing Galbraith's model to the organization's unique needs and identifying the specific projects that addressed these needs. Given how extensive the work was with this top team, I offer snapshots of three initiatives from the twelve-month journey.

Improved Partnering with the New CEO

The prior CEO managed external stakeholder relationships, leaving nearly all the organization's functioning to his senior staff. The new CEO preferred a much more hands-on role in leading the business. The senior team was expected to work together closely, focused on cross-functional operational improvements.

Individual consultations with each executive strengthened these relationships. The COO's aim was to mutually define expectations with the CEO. The CEO was dissatisfied with information system performance. In response, the IT head's work was aimed at implementing service-level agreements with his internal customers. The CFO, a profound introvert, was used to largely being left alone to do his work. The new CEO was interested in partnering much more closely as they jointly built a new budget for the much larger enterprise they would be leading.

The use of "valentines" was another tactic used to enhance the CEO's relationships with his direct reports. The name came from the saying, "When you care enough to send the very best ... and that's the truth!" This method was invented by my mentor Kathie Dannemiller and colleagues in their work to foster cross-functional collaboration at Ford.[14] Each member of the senior team completed one-page feedback sheets for one another, answering questions about patterns of behavior they experienced, the impact these had on them, and stop-start-continue requests going forward. Ultimately these valentines led the entire organization to develop a Code of Conduct to guide all internal and external relationships.

Better Meetings

A subgroup of the leadership team took on the task of reinventing the business's meetings. The group's early recommendations included an item that received unanimous support: "Define the purpose of each meeting and each agenda item before discussions begin." Was the item just an FYI? Did the item's "owner" want input? Or maybe an exploration was all that was needed to better understand an issue. The final type of agenda item was that a decision had to be made. The favorite change made to meetings was the invention of a Get out of Meeting card everyone could play if no meeting purpose and agenda was circulated twenty-four hours before its start time. The practice of defining the purpose and agenda before meetings began to be followed throughout the operation, an example of how Applying One Lever had positive impact in this story, as there was no formal change program for the whole company.

Complex Board–Staff Decisions and a Real-Time Redesign Opportunity

The board and staff had experienced some unproductive meetings since the new CEO had taken the helm. Although not an original part of the project plan, an opportunity to work on these issues arose. With the new expansion, the board and staff faced a series of important decisions regarding the master plan for growth. How could the staff convey the sophistication needed for smart, strategic decisions to be made?

In response, the staff literally created a puzzle of the decisions. The puzzle illustrated how some decisions were interdependent, some impacted others, and a few were independent and could be made without ramifications to other elements of the plan. Senior staff had found a way to describe the complexity of the master plan without oversimplifying it. These opportunistic conversations went a long way toward improving the relationship between the two groups.

The Design It Yourself lever gives you both the possibility and charge to craft your own change effort. We own what we help create. Having your organization create its own change effort means that people will own the outcomes of the effort, too. Get clear about your purpose and outcomes. Chart your organization's course forward. Pay attention to progress made and where your original plans may be falling short of the mark, and be prepared to make changes along the way. This lever is about making sure that your change work is done for reasons you believe in, defined by you, and done by you. It's the best way to stack the odds in your favor from the start.

HOW TO KNOW YOU'VE APPLIED THIS LEVER WELL

• You have a shared picture of your organization's past and present.

• Anyone can understand your purpose, outcomes, and road map.

• Your road map will achieve your purpose and outcomes, and your purpose and outcomes respond to your current realities.

• There are unique elements of your change effort that fit the distinctive aspects of your organization.

4

CREATE A COMMON DATABASE

People make decisions and take actions every day in your organization. The quality of shared understanding drives the effectiveness of these decisions and actions. Your eventual success rests with the number of the people who deeply understand what you're trying to accomplish, why, how, and what their role is in making it happen. Information in organizations was once seen to be a source of power over others. Create a Common Database is about having power *with* others. The more you share needed information, the more valuable it becomes ... and the more powerful your people. Better, easier, and faster results come from aligned action. Aligned action finds its home in a common database.

A Common Problem: People Don't Know Enough to Make Good Decisions

Leaders often don't believe that people lower in the organization can make good, strategic decisions. They complain that these others don't appreciate market complexities, enterprise-wide financial implications, or emerging technologies. When people lower in the hierarchy are trusted to make decisions with far-reaching implications, they appear to leaders to be out of touch with reality. When poor (read: uninformed) decisions are made, leaders sometimes complain that there's been too much participation. At the surface, this logic appears sound. And therein lies the crux of the issue. Without access to needed information, how can anyone make smart, considered decisions?

People on the front lines have their own concerns. They don't believe leaders understand the organization's daily operations. They object to direction from above because leaders appear to them to have their heads in the clouds, seduced by big-picture thinking and the tantalizing promise of a strategy lacking only effective implementation.

Managers in the middle have long been labeled as the source of communication problems in most organizations. Information comes to them from the top and bottom of the business, and often stays there. Even when information makes it throughout an organization, the kind of insight available only through deeper dialogues is missing. Promises of a better future become hollow when information is exchanged but meaning is lost.

These same issues rear their head across the hierarchy. What about situations when the voice of the customer is brought forward by a sales organization? Too often, the production side of the house is stuck with unrealistic promises made to buyers. Lacking appreciation of each other's timing, needed customer features, or other competing priorities, two internal units can get embroiled in negotiations that devolve into unproductive debates and differences of opinion.

Solution: Create a Common Database

The Create a Common Database lever is the remedy to these problems of people not knowing enough to make good decisions. Named by my mentor Kathie Dannemiller, it busts the paradigm in which information represents power for a few. Those advocating sharing information on a "need to know" basis have not always been far off the mark. It's just that their definition of who needs to know has woefully undercounted those in need of strategic information. This lever argues that we should err on the side of disclosing more information to more people. Challenges posed by a hierarchy, a matrix, or demanding customer needs are no match for an organization focused on a free flow of information up, down, and across. This lever also acknowledges the importance of inquiring minds that dig deeper for understanding and of people who advocate for their point of view. Both of these approaches lead to more data being available to the entire organization.

Know also that creating a common database is not about ensuring these understandings exist at only a single point in time. You need to find ways to keep now-common knowledge common over time. New realities emerge, requiring a culture of learning backed by conversations, processes, systems, and structures that support this new way of doing business. Whether in individual conversations, team meetings, or large group gatherings, you need to find ways to deploy the Create a Common Database lever.

STORY

We once held a series of large group meetings around the world for a company that had recently undergone a merger. The business deal required complex financing—intricate enough to qualify as a topic in an MBA course. Frontline workers typically would not have the details of the deal explained to them. After all, why did they need to know about the convertible debt and floating interest rates? The premise of Create a Common Database is that the more everyone knows what everyone knows, the more informed, strategic decisions get made by all. Thousands of decisions are made every day in organizations that are either aligned or not aligned with the company's future direction. The less aligned they are, the more friction is created in getting from point A to point B. In the case of this company, explaining the complicated financing of the deal helped people understand the huge benefits of accelerating production timelines to beat the bond due dates. Information was power ... shared with all.

How This Lever Helps Create Faster, Easier, Better Results

This lever ensures that everyone in an organization makes smart decisions in line with the company's overall strategy. Every choice made everywhere by everybody deserves to benefit from a broad base of information. You achieve faster, easier, better results in change work by applying this lever, for the following six reasons:

1. *The need for change makes sense to all.* There are many facets to a change story. Each person has their own perspective. Each perspective leads to a more complete appreciation of the entire effort. When your part of the puzzle gets connected to the parts of others, you better understand the whole by appreciating the relationships among the pieces. That understanding translates into time and energy being devoted to helping the whole instead of just taking care of your part.

2. *Better decisions are made every day everywhere.* More understanding enhances the quality of conclusions reached from the executive suite to the shop floor. Debates about right and wrong get replaced by conversations about what makes the most

sense. Trade-offs get weighed; implications are explored. Choices and plans of action are reached based on solid logic, not just the prerogative of the most powerful person in the room.

3. *Your organization becomes the home of strategic thinkers.* Organizations that use the Create a Common Database lever are on the lookout for what's new and different. Anomalies aren't easily explained away as isolated instances. Surface-level answers get a more thorough review through the efforts of people digging deeper to bring to light long-held assumptions. Explanations that make sense to all become a common goal.

4. *Organizational intelligence increases.* Organizations that focus on learning are smarter than those that don't. People understand not just what they do but also *why* they do what they do. Just as emotional intelligence measures how well people are in touch with their feelings,[15] organizational intelligence defines how well people understand how their entity operates. Change becomes faster, easier, and better when you understand why things work the way they do at some times—and why they don't at others.

5. *Changes are no longer made in one part of the organization without other parts knowing.* People connect the dots. The extra question always gets asked: "How will the changes we are making affect other groups?" Actions are no longer taken in isolation. Prevention becomes the name of the game instead of finding and fixing disconnects after changes have already been implemented.

6. *Learning and curiosity take the place of defensiveness.* In too many cases, ensuring accountability results in having someone to point a finger at when things go wrong. How many celebrations were thrown for accountable parties in your organization in the recent past? A client of mine emphasized how blame had become an odd core competence, referring to the saying "We want one throat to choke" when things go wrong. Learning is something that is done together. Problems are identified and resolved faster when time isn't wasted looking for the guilty party to blame for a mistake.

Success Factors in Applying This Lever

Want to gain the greatest advantage from applying this lever? Put the following five factors in place and reap the benefits afforded an aligned organization capable of taking insightful actions.

Factor One: Include Both Internal and External Information

Understanding how and why the organization operates as it does is just as important as having your finger on the pulse of the external environment. You never know what could accelerate or derail your change work. Are there other internal initiatives occurring that need to be connected to yours? What about what's happening in the rapidly changing world around you? The learning you do is only as good as the information you're basing it on. Continue looking for clues, especially after you think you have a handle on your situation. Know there are inevitable surprises in your future. Don't be caught off guard.

Factor Two: Pay Attention to Both Facts and Feelings

Most organizations favor facts over feelings. Facts are objective. You can measure and track them. They're an essential piece of an organization's puzzle. Yet alone they are not enough. How people feel about things matters too. Harder to count or tabulate to be sure. It's the subjective realm, but equally valid. Are people excited about changes you're making—or afraid of them? Are they confident or concerned? People's energy, their discretionary effort, is governed by the soft side of the measuring stick. Don't find yourself favoring facts or feelings over the other. They both count.

Factor Three: Put Processes in Place for Sustaining Learning over Time

It's not going to be enough to assume that once your organization knows how to learn, it will remember how to do it again. You need to practice and get better over time. A good process will enable a person to perform above their given competence level. The same is true for organizations. Good information-sharing processes will ensure that this valuable element of change work is not treated like a once-and-done task.

Factor Four: Learn How to Communicate Effectively through Both Inquiry and Advocacy

Learning is about your becoming informed by others and their gaining insights from you. It's no better to hide your opinion than to not seek out another's. The healthiest relationships, whether personal or organizational, are grounded in mutual understanding. The deeper and more meaningful the conversation, the greater the learning that occurs. Every organization I've ever consulted with has had a "communication problem." (Doesn't yours too?)

I believe that the source of these problems lies in an inability to genuinely be curious about others' perspectives while at the same time taking a strong stance in support of one's own. Doing both at the same time can be tricky business. Leverage this polarity well, and you're well ahead of your competition. Overfocus on the other person, and you risk being seen as hiding your own opinions. Expound too much on your point of view, and you can easily get labeled as someone who works their own agenda at others' expense. Strike the right balance in your own behavior, and your team's, and you've hit the sweet spot of learning.

Factor Five: Pay Attention to Different Perspectives about the Same Information

Don't underestimate the value of discovering different points of view about what appears at face value to be the same information. Understanding what led to the perceptions of each party will ensure that you make wise decisions about what to sustain or improve in the future. Learning occurs when people feel free to share their thoughts—no matter how bizarre they may seem to the rest of the group assembled. Affirm the outliers. Guard against shutting down conversation too soon. Rushing to judgment is the enemy of Create a Common Database. Find ways to become more comfortable tolerating ambiguity and even confusion. The most valuable learning can result from the most awkward conversations.

STORY

My friend and colleague Jennifer Brown has dedicated her life to advancing the essential work of diversity, equity, and inclusion (DEI) in organizations. She and her colleagues were working with a financial services company interested in expanding their Employee Resource Groups (ERGs.) ERGs represent people from different backgrounds and identities and provide much-needed community, as well as consultation to companies on business issues, such as how to best enter markets; develop new, more inclusive product features; and improve recruitment strategies. Examples of ERGs include race and ethnicity-focused groups and LGBTQ+ communities.

The financial services company wanted to create a new ERG focused on people with disabilities. This group formed through a combination of internal survey data in which an estimated 30 percent of the professional population identified as having a disability of some type. There were also individual requests to form such a group and a senior executive who wanted to sponsor the work. The organization had also gathered information through exit interviews, public employment forums on the web, and anecdotal feedback from recruited candidates that reinforced the importance of this group.

The business became aware that hidden disabilities weren't being considered in common situations and often remained under the organizational waterline due to associated stigma. Previously, as in most organizations, it wasn't unusual for a presenter at an internal meeting to ask whether people could hear them adequately in the room, then quickly putting the microphone aside for their own comfort. Input from the People with Disabilities ERG revealed that employees with low hearing felt stigmatized and weren't comfortable expressing in the moment their need for the mic. This led to a new practice whereby microphones were used in all larger group gatherings. Like so many accessible design strategies, utilizing microphones at all times doesn't just assist those who are deaf but assists all of us in our ability to follow, listen, and comprehend.

ERGs are a great strategy for taking advantage of the Create a Common Database lever. They open opportunities for previously underrepresented employees to have their voices heard in shaping business plans, product development strategies, and innovative approaches to employee retention. In the story here, strategic information shared in meetings was unknowingly not even being received by all employees until the new ERG was created and began to use its collective voice to educate. Lessons learned through these powerful DEI groups become organizational wisdom with far-reaching benefits for employees, the companies in which they work, and the customers they serve.

How to Know You've Applied This Lever Well

How do you know you've done a good job of deploying the Create a Common Database lever? Work your way through the items here, ensuring a yes on every dimension, and you'll be well on your way to achieving faster, easier, better results.

People in the Organization Are Creating Integrated Views

Meeting this standard is not about convincing others that you are right and they are wrong. Are people who traditionally hold different views able to tell a cohesive story about the reality they are experiencing? Making this possible affords you the chance to reveal unexpected consequences as well as to confirm obvious conclusions. In one client engagement, we were confronted with a set of issues between design engineers (who worked at corporate headquarters) and plant engineers (who worked on the factory floor). The two groups had different goals, did different work, and had different backgrounds. Alone they were left to bicker, each side convinced it was right. And they each were. But only partially right. Together, by educating each other, they learned how the whole system worked and where the breakdowns occurred. The causes of their misunderstandings became clearer. An integrated view is a more complete view—one that leads to more informed, and better, decisions.

New Information Makes Its Way throughout the Organization

The free and open flow of communication is another sign that this lever is being applied well. One way information can be shared in your organization is through systems that house data from multiple parts of the business (e.g., production, sales, HR). Another is through meetings especially designed to widen the circle of communication, or even through informal conversations. How many gatherings have you attended lately with the express purpose of creating common understandings? Are the lessons learned in one part of the business shared with others? When you've successfully used the Create a Common Database lever, you can answer yes to these questions. The default assumption is that something can be learned from any situation, shared, and used to improve operations in ways that will benefit the whole. If you think you have a unique set of circumstances that won't be relevant to anyone else in the organization, think again. You can't predict where or how your lessons will be helpful to others. Start by assuming that your experience will be valuable to others instead of believing that it's a special case.

People Have Solid Reasons for Decisions They Make

When this lever is in place, people know the "why" behind what they're doing. They've tested hypotheses about what's gone right and wrong—and why these scenarios have played out differently. I often have clients prove their case in the "Court of Change." It's a fun way to deal with potentially serious issues. Pretend you have opposing counsels. One argues for the changes you're contemplating, the other against. How does the case for change and the argument the counsel is making align with the overall strategy of the organization? What does the evidence tell you? If you had to prove your case to a jury, in whose favor would the court rule, and why? It's no longer acceptable to hold "I think, you think" debates where long-held assumptions on each side are used as evidence of a compelling argument. The merits of the "case" rule the day. No decision is too large or too small to get this treatment. Actions are taken based on the strongest logic ... and that logic has been well vetted by those charged with implementing those actions.

Implications Are Explored before Action Is Taken

People in organizations focused on this lever play with possibilities. They look at scenarios and assess probabilities. They are ready for multiple responses from the marketplace. They reward patience and value the extra question. Interestingly, another sign of Create a Common Database is that people make rapid modifications to accommodate new realities. They've already thought through and debated various paths forward. There are few unexpected consequences. It's like playing chess and thinking three moves ahead. The drive to action can be hard to resist. Does that call need to be made right now ... or will soon be good enough? You have more time to study alternatives if you make the time to do it. There's no room for a "My way or the highway" approach when common understanding is truly valued. "Our way" becomes the best way.

Examples of This Lever in Action

An automotive manufacturer and a telecom provider make sure that people in their organizations use Create a Common Database. Different paths for different organizations, with the same outcome: informed, aligned companies aimed at achieving their overall strategies.

STORY: GLADS, SADS, AND MADS

We were working with an automotive manufacturer whose finance and production units had been experiencing the same problem for years. The monthly roll-up of financial statements could never be completed fast enough for the numbers people. Their chief nemesis in this conflict, plant personnel, regularly complained that they had product to get out the door. What difference did it make if the numbers waited another day or two?

We used a Glads, Sads, and Mads brainstorm activity developed by Ron Lippitt, a pioneer in the field of organization change, as a way to include people's emotions in an analysis of their organization's performance.[16] Venting and celebrating occur at the same time. One person's glad can be another's mad. It's a fast way to help people appreciate that their opinions aren't the only valid ones in the world. Even when there isn't agreement, it's tough to ignore someone else's experience, especially when they're sitting right next to you. The freedom to focus on new product launches ended up on the Glad list for people from the plants, while that very same "freedom" landed on the Mad list for members of the finance team. Flip charts quickly filled, some with agreed-on points, others reflecting how the two groups were at odds.

The key to this activity, and Create a Common Database, was that neither side had to change the other's mind. Different realities existed for different parts of the organization. By seeing this dynamic in real time, everyone came to appreciate one another's point of view. Getting the launch of a new vehicle right on time and within the given budget was a win for the whole company. Having the quarterly reports finished gave the finance people time to prepare for earnings calls. Seeing this issue from everyone's perspective didn't solve it. Why this cycle repeated itself every quarter became clearer. The organization's design pitted these groups against each other. Neither was the enemy. Learning this together made it possible for the groups to set boundaries and decision criteria that everyone could agree on. Having learned about one another's perspectives, they were better able to roll up their sleeves and work together.

STORY: CHANGE POSSIBILITIES PANELS

A ten-thousand-person telecom company was facing stiff competition. It had operated with the benefit of captive customers, not needing to innovate services or how they were delivered. However, these new ideas were keys to the business's future success. We were asked to support an effort that would bring the company's culture in line with its new, fast-paced strategy. There were pockets of progress in the company, places where the new culture had taken hold. The product development lab had recently been expanded and was off and running. The pipeline was filling up with new hardware, but the rest of the organization continued to operate in the Dark Ages.

People needed to know more about the good work already unfolding as part of the effort and how they could build on it. These were important lessons to be shared with the rest of the organization, and this was done in meetings both large and small. Presenters did not tell others what they needed to do to succeed. Each situation and part of the company would need unique solutions. Instead, the presentations described lessons learned so that insights about how to create change in one part of the business could be capitalized on in another. These sessions also led to increased optimism as people gained a deeper appreciation of progress being made and the reasons underlying these early successes.

These sessions, known as Change Possibilities Panels (first developed for use at Ford Motor Company in the mid-1980s[17]), are a powerful approach to Create a Common Database. It's important that panel members only share their own experiences, not give directives. People get defensive when they're told the right way to do something. These panels are not about people having answers; instead, they're focused on questions:

- Why did you do what you did?
- What impact did your decisions have on others?
- How did you measure success?
- What kinds of resources were needed?
- What was most exciting, and where were you frustrated?

A Change Possibilities Panel recognizes and rewards those who have taken chances and proceeded into uncertain territory. This encourages others to experiment. Don't worry about finding the one best way; there are many paths forward. What worked for members of the panel may or may not work for you. The process of exploring, testing, learning, and retesting is what is important.

What knowledge do you have to share that could add value for others in the work they do? Don't forget to ask what they know that might benefit you. A common database is the swiftest and surest path to an aligned organization. Identify the information needed for your effort to succeed and ensure that it gets shared early, often, and widely.

HOW TO KNOW YOU'VE APPLIED THIS LEVER WELL

❑ People in the organization are creating integrated views.

❑ New information makes its way throughout the organization.

❑ People have solid reasons for decisions they make.

❑ Implications are explored before action is taken.

5

START WITH IMPACT, FOLLOW THE ENERGY

Making changes can be hard. Some people don't understand why change is needed. Others know why it's needed, but don't know what to do to make it happen. A third group knows what's needed to make change happen, but they just don't want to do it. Aren't those differences enough of a challenge for one change effort? Now, on top of that, take away any choice about where people are to begin their work ... and what to do next. Insist that it has to start at the top and cascade through the organization level by level. There's another way forward, one that's powerful and appropriate for any situation you're facing: Start with Impact, Follow the Energy.

A Common Problem: All Change Efforts Must Begin from the Top

Where can you find the rule that all change must begin at the top? Probably in every book you've ever picked up on organizations and change. Commitment from senior leaders is on the must-have list. A guiding coalition needs to provide direction for the overall effort. Executives need to "walk the talk" before expecting anyone else to get on board in making needed changes.

Leaders have four choices when it comes to change: Lead. Support. Allow. Or block. In my experience, few senior leaders actively block needed change in their organizations. Senior executive support from the start makes the work easier, to be sure. This lever is especially helpful when, for whatever reason, senior leaders aren't prepared to get out in front of your change work.

Solution: Start with Impact, Follow the Energy

Rather than following the rule of starting at the top, let's begin with a question: What is going to help the organization move toward its preferred future, faster? Maybe it *is* starting at the top. I've worked with many organizations that have taken that approach and been successful. But if that's your only way forward, you're missing opportunities that may be a better fit for your situation. Don't lock yourself into a one-size-fits-all mindset. Requiring senior leaders to be fully committed and to point the way from the start can stop your change effort before it's even begun.

There are also choices about how to proceed once you've started. Most common is the cascade approach, where each level in the organization follows its leaders. Then the group that has just followed, leads its followers. And so on. This model is based on the premise that one has to be converted oneself before converting others.

Here's another paradigm. It's one of energy and following where the work takes you. What new possibilities for progress open up after you've taken the last step? Where does it make sense to veer off your charted course because there is value to be gained faster, easier, and better than originally planned? Blindly following a top-down strategy is no better than automatically opting for a grassroots approach. Both can work ... and there are other choices. Work where you can. Work where progress is most needed. Work where you'll open doors to advances that will make a big difference. Maybe it makes sense to go where it'll be less costly. Or where you can easily build momentum. Pay attention to the work that wants to happen.

You can begin in the middle, top, bottom, side, or center of an organization. To paraphrase

Kurt Lewin, the father of modern social psychology, the best way to understand a system is to try to change it.[18] You'll learn by moving forward—from any starting point. Where you go next should depend on what you've learned along the way.

STORY

A technology products company was undergoing a major reorganization. The changes had been recommended by a cross-functional task force and approved by the executive team. How the changes were going to be implemented was still an open discussion. One thing was known: change was going to affect the whole organization. Using a traditional paradigm, it would have made sense to begin working with the senior leadership, form a steering committee to oversee the effort, and get buy-in from all key stakeholders before beginning. However, a leader in the sales organization was eager to get his team operating at peak performance from day 1. He was ready, willing, and able. The sales department was a key leverage point for the organization-wide change effort. The changes in sales were going to affect nearly every other department in the company. We began our work with this group. This work didn't start at the top; it began in the middle. It made sense to leverage the sales leader's energy and commitment. His team was on board too, leading to an early, strategic win that would eventually affect the entire organization. In this case, starting at the top with a formal rollout would have slowed things down.

How This Lever Helps Create Faster, Easier, Better Results

I first learned about the thinking behind this lever from my friend and colleague Myron Rogers. Myron's wisdom challenges the All Change Efforts Must Begin at the Top mantra. You can achieve faster, easier, better results in your change work by applying this lever, for the following five reasons:

1. *Start where change is easy ... or where it's hard.* It's straightforward to begin where it's easy. Why bother with the hard path? Choosing the easy route will take less time, money, and energy. You can probably also make more progress sooner. But where change is hard, it could be worth the extra effort needed. Imagine if you could succeed

where the going is tough. You'll earn the respect of those who have yet to make up their minds. You may even find that what you thought was going to be the hard path turns out to be the easy one—or vice versa. The best question to ask is, "How can I most effectively get where I need to go?"

2. *Work with energy—whether it's positive or negative.* Following positive energy seems obvious. It's easy to build momentum and move forward when people see you making progress in creating the future they desire. You can even create virtuous cycles of initial commitment and motivation that lead to even more dedication and enthusiasm over time. But what about negative energy? Negative energy is not the opposite of positive. Apathy is. When people don't care, creating change is like trying to push a rope uphill. Groups perceived to have negative attitudes about change get labeled resisters, people who won't get on board, or just plain troublemakers. Ironically, these naysayers may have even greater commitment than groups with so-called positive energy. They appear to be pessimistic, but maybe that's because of your point of view. Shifting energy is far

easier than creating it. You'll often find that these mischief makers become your greatest champions for change over time.

3. *What you learn early, you can apply later.* There is no perfect opening move when it comes to change. Which option will be most strategic, have the highest impact, or give you the best return on investment? Consider these questions, but at the same time don't get seduced into grand debates that interfere with beginning your work. You'll learn along the way and make course corrections over time. Here are some other questions to think through early on:

• Who may be quiet leaders in the organization you may not have noticed before?

• Who could be strong followers providing needed energy along the way?

• What's worked so far that you want to capitalize on going forward?

• What hasn't worked that you want to avoid in the future?

Your change work will improve by applying lessons learned, regardless of where you begin your work and however you follow it forward.

4. *Work in many parts of the organization at once.* No one says that you must work in only one part of the organization at a time.

What you try in one place may help you in another. What you learn in one area, you can apply in another. Maybe launch five or six initiatives at the same time, or decide you need to focus on only one or two. It's your call. Try doing different kinds of work in different parts of the organization. What insights can you gain from the variety of approaches you're using? What tactics pay the fastest dividends? Which have the biggest returns on investment? Keep your central question front and center: What will yield faster, easier, better results?

5. *Don't buy the argument that cascading is best because you ensure that everyone has the same experience.* Maybe everybody doesn't need the same experience. With Start with Impact, Follow the Energy you can customize your work. What you do is driven by what makes sense given the realities you're facing, not by some lockstep plan of working level by level through the hierarchy. Your path may surprise even you—in a good way. Pay attention to the work you're drawn to do with people who are drawn to do that work. Trust that people know the experiences they need to move from point A to point B. If you can let go of your preconceived plans, you'll be

able to follow people's motivation, excitement, and bias for action, which will guide you along the way.

Success Factors in Applying This Lever

There is great freedom with the Start with Impact, Follow the Energy lever, and along with it comes some risk. Reduce any threats to the success of your change work by putting the following five success factors in place.

Factor One: Have Your Finger on the Pulse of the Organization

To follow the flow of energy in your organization, you need to know where the energy exists. Understand what's happening at levels above and below you. This means that people have to be straight with you, and you need to be honest in return. Have authentic conversations with others about your own hopes and fears. "Good soldiers" will tell you what they think you want to hear. Good insights don't come from bad data. Make sure people feel safe talking to you—especially in the difficult conversations. Take time to understand the real reasons that people feel the way they do. As you listen, also test hypotheses about why things are the way they are. Soon you'll be able to predict how people will answer your questions because you've listened carefully to their colleagues. That's when you'll know you've got a good read of what's happening in the organization.

Factor Two: Do the Work That Needs to Be Done—Not Always the Work You Planned to Do

Barbara Bunker, a mentor of mine, once told me long ago, "Structure is helpful. It gives you something to deviate from." Have a solid plan. At the same time, don't be fooled by having to follow it. New opportunities to achieve faster, easier, better results will emerge from the work you are doing. Sometimes following your original plan is your best course of action, but don't do so blindly. Remember how you've defined success. What moves you closer to that goal is the work you need to be doing. Here's a way to keep yourself honest: Test assumptions as you go. Have an educated guess about where you expect people to be at certain points in time. See how close your expectations are to reality. Test yourself to keep your bearings:

- Where are we in achieving our desired results?
- Where did we expect to be at this time?
- What level of understanding, clarity, and commitment did we expect to have at this point in the process, and are we there?

Sometimes new work will emerge that, if done well, will make your path forward smarter.

Factor Three: Make Sure That Leadership Is Willing to Trust the Process

Are leaders genuinely committed to employing this lever? There's nothing worse than people thinking they have the freedom to move forward as they see fit, only to be pulled up short by a leader who has another view of the right way to go. Start with Impact, Follow the Energy represents a paradigm shift for most leaders. Deviating from the project plan is not always seen to be good management practice. However, trusting the process is not the same as being excluded from it. Leaders need to be part of early explorations into better paths to pursue. They need to become change agents, not just providers of guidance for others' change efforts. Make some leaders members of the team designing your change. If they are only people to whom the team reports, leaders are stuck in the role of critic, relegated to either praising or criticizing work that's already done.

Factor Four: Be Opportunistic and Planful

An overly opportunistic approach makes it feel as though everything is up for grabs, and you're chasing every shiny object as a potential difference maker. Be too planful, and people feel constrained by the road map, not guided by it. What are signs that you're taking advantage of being both opportunistic and planful in the right doses?

- You discover unexpected chances to build momentum by capturing wins that had previously gone unnoticed.
- Newly discovered allies put their shoulders to the wheel, adding much-needed energy to make work easier to complete.
- You see and take advantage of synergies between different initiatives that have a multiplier effect on progress.
- Rocks in the river are identified far upstream and problems prevented; you no longer have to find and fix mistakes after they've been made.

When you use this lever well, you'll reap the benefits of both strategies and minimize the costs of overfocusing on either.

Factor Five: Don't Let Your Own Agenda Be (the Only) Driver in the Process

Let's say you sound clearer than others about how to proceed. You've thought more about this change work. There are good reasons for what you're proposing. You tell a compelling story. Be careful! The only way Start with Impact, Follow the Energy works is if the organization helps determine how fast things move and in what direction. Don't let your own well-considered plans get in the way. Introduce them, but don't be swayed by your own comfort level. Another mentor of mine and a giant in the field of social sciences, Ken Benne, once said to me, "When you are most certain of the way forward is when you most need to step back and question it again." If you're having trouble welcoming new perspectives, that's an early warning sign. Clarity is good. But pay attention to whether the clarity you're sensing is yours alone or the organization's. Make sure at the end of the day that it's the organization pointing the way to its future.

STORY

A large retail chain needed to rapidly implement a new strategy to significantly grow market share. The change work began in the center of the organization and expanded from there. Internal buyers were going to be key players in the success of the strategy. They were the first line of relationships with the supply chain that needed to expand to meet the business's growth needs. We started with a one-day meeting for 150 of these buyers to understand the strategy, improve it, and define their roles in making it happen. Three weeks later, multiple work teams were up and running on initiatives developed in the launch meeting. Merchandisers, those promoting sales through their presentation in retail outlets, were next in line. These were the buyers' natural internal partners. We also held a one-day strategy introduction meeting for them to plan how they could best jump on the organization's moving train.

After these teams were launched, we held a "roles and responsibilities" summit with the buying and merchandising groups. At that gathering, the teams made promises to each other about the work they each would do, support they would provide the other, and processes they would put in place immediately to manage the upcoming expanded workload. Senior executives had been involved in all work to this point, but had yet to convene their own dedicated retreat.

Only at this point, three months after the first work in the organization, did the senior leadership team hold a formal change meeting. In it they decided on how they could best provide support moving forward. After this retreat, a three-day organization-wide meeting was held to introduce a set of new accelerated work practices. People then redefined their work to fast-track implementation of the new practices.

Two months on the heels of this large group event, where the idea of an organization-wide training center was generated, the center was opened to develop competencies needed for the new organization to succeed. Two months later, a new set of processes was introduced at another organization-wide multiday meeting. Gains were solidified and a growth mindset was normalized in this gathering. The business continued on its growth trajectory, earning a mention in the larger company's annual report for its wins in expanding its footprint. An unconventional, emergent road map for change started where there were opportunities for impact and followed the energy from there.

How to Know You've Applied This Lever Well

You began your change work in one place and followed it to another. You've heeded the advice of this lever, but how well have you done it? Review the next sections and check yourself against the list at the end of the chapter to assess your success.

You Have Good Reasons for Starting Where You Have—and for Going Where You've Gone

The freedom to finally start your effort where you want and to move forward in ways that make sense can feel great. To know you've done well, you need to have a coherent argument for why you're doing things the way you are. Be able to describe your thinking and rationale in plain terms that are easily understood. Have conversations about how your work has progressed, highlighting what you've done *and why you've done it.* Be clear about these reasons with yourself and others. This lever is not an invitation to do whatever you want. You should be able to construct a clear, convincing argument. If you can't, go back and find a path where you can.

Change Pulls You through the Organization—You're Not Trying to Push It Forward

We all know what it feels like to be rowing upstream against resistance, every pull of the oar harder than the last. Sometimes resistance is active, showing up as arguments in favor of the status quo. In other cases, it's passive, with people adopting a "This too shall pass" attitude. Following the energy in an organization makes things easier to accomplish. People welcome your support in making needed changes. You and others experience higher and higher levels of trust and excitement about the collective future you are creating. Progress becomes easier; you have the energy of the organization working for you instead of against you.

At Some Point along the Way, You Find Yourself Surprised about Where You're Working, with Whom, or on What

The odds of getting every step right from the get-go are slim to none. If you're following your plan exactly as you laid it out, consider the possibility that you may be more locked in on your plan than in creating faster, easier, better results. Changing organizations don't follow a straight line from point A to point B. Winds and currents shift, as do people's attitudes and the progress of initiatives linked to your change work. As you discover opportunities for impact, you clarify new work, and different partners emerge. Your position relative to the destination is all that matters. It's not important where you're working in the organization, with whom, and on what. The only thing that matters is your getting closer to where you want and need to be.

More and More, You Are Working with People Who Are More and More Energized

People want to do work that needs to be done. When you're on the right path, it's not as hard to get volunteers to step up and make things happen. Positive energy is contagious. Encouragement takes the place of criticism as one good idea leads to another. A successful initiative makes another possible. You can feel the tide turning. Informal conversations, previously taking the form of a rumor mill filled with complaints, are transformed. People now take notice of progress made to date. More of the organization wants to get involved, finding ways to use their expertise for the greater good. People are excited to be part of something larger than themselves. The further you advance your cause, the larger this confident crowd becomes. You've tapped into the limitless supply of positive energy in your organization.

You've Explored Different Scenarios and Trade-Offs along the Way

A good way to make sure you're on the right path is to know where you could have taken a few wrong turns—or even to have taken some, learned from them, and found your way back on track. You should know the potential costs you might have to pay and the benefits you could gain from following various road maps. The goal is to make informed decisions about the most promising directions to pursue. Imagine the results you could achieve. Take the time to also identify the unexpected consequences of different routes. Don't get trapped with only one way forward. Come up with options. Assess the time, money, and energy required for different ones and make decisions that will serve you best.

Examples of This Lever in Action

Following are two very different stories of applying the Start with Impact, Follow the Energy lever. The first describes a two-year change effort that started with a half-day problem-solving session at a utility; the second is the story of an industrial automation company that took advantage of a fresh perspective on all-too-common problems. A new culture and the use of a new concept were each an aim of two very different organizations. They both began in one place within the organization and followed an interesting path to others. Both of them eventually created system-wide impact.

STORY: A HALF-DAY PROBLEM-SOLVING SESSION AS THE BEGINNING OF A TWO-YEAR TRANSFORMATION EFFORT

I got a request one day to plan and facilitate a half-day problem-solving session. It was to take place at a ten-thousand-person utility company that had just suffered major layoffs. At face value, a half day wasn't going to make much difference, given the issues facing the company. What was less clear was what might become possible if we responded to this request and saw where it could go.

Eighty people had been invited to the working session. We met with the business line leaders, one of whom said that he had heard that I was disappointed that more people weren't invited. I told him that having more people attending would improve the quality of the work and enhance the odds of rapidly implementing new ideas—not the solution to all their problems, but change would occur fast enough to send a message that things could be done differently going forward. The next week, we opened the meeting to a crowd of three hundred. The conveners were already looking for ways to increase the impact. The large group did good work, even if limited in scope.

The CEO came to hear the final reports and close the meeting. As he stood in front of the group, the first thing he said was, "Wow!" His experience of that meeting opened his mind to the possibility of a group that large arriving at decisions to improve the company. This was the beginning.

To take advantage of this insight, the senior executives invited a cross section of the entire business to a three-day meeting—five hundred people in all. Before this gathering, the executives drafted a new mission, vision, and values for the business. They asked the large group to provide feedback on their draft and develop immediate "difference-making" actions. This event was followed by another where eight hundred people gathered for two days to translate the mission, vision, and values into daily actions and behaviors to be implemented throughout the enterprise. These ideas led to redesigned work processes, changes in how they set strategy, and improved management and union interactions.

We started where we could and followed the company's energy into a two-year effort that transformed the organization from a noncompetitor in its market to a leader in innovation and customer satisfaction.

STORY: HOW INTRODUCING POLARITY THINKING TO AN HR EXECUTIVE TEAM OPENED THE DOOR FOR ORGANIZATION-WIDE CHANGE

We once worked with a global industrial automation and information technology company of twenty-three thousand. This story is an excellent example of how Applying One Lever—Start with Impact, Follow the Energy—led to organization-wide change. Our work was never part of a formal change program, yet the power of this lever led to large-scale changes in how the organization operated.

The project began with an annual strategy session with the senior HR executives. We followed that gathering with an expanded HR team meeting aimed at advancing strategies developed in the first meeting. Polarity Thinking was integrated as a core element of each gathering. Internal customers of the HR organization were intrigued with the idea of polarities, and used this model when they engaged in further action planning.

We responded to this interest in a number of ways. An internal affinity group focusing on diversity hosted a meeting where Polarity Thinking was introduced and applied to underlying issues the group was working on. The affinity group's mission was to help create a new, more diverse, and welcoming organization. Seeing through a polarity lens, they came to appreciate the pole of business performance and changed their mission to "Create a new, more diverse, welcoming, and successful organization."

Senior executives used the polarity paradigm to plan the corporation's overall strategy in more detail. A special task force focused on diffusing innovative practices throughout the company leveraged their new understanding of polarities to identify breakthrough plans that would radically accelerate their timelines and deliverables. We made a special presentation to the top two hundred global leaders in a quarterly operations meeting. The leaders were then asked to take the new way of thinking home and apply it to their own organization's challenges. Two business units used polarity tools to resolve a conflict about whether to keep high inventories so that customers had more choices or to maintain low ones to manage costs.

A polarity point of view was disseminated throughout this organization in a matter of months. There was no preconceived plan to expand thinking in the organization. We started with the HR organization, and as other parts of the business found polarities useful, we followed their lead. Work begun with a simple annual strategy offsite for the senior HR team evolved into a system-wide change effort.

Starting where there is impact calls for a different mindset than the traditional "start at the top" worldview. It requires you to assess probabilities of success and explore cost-benefit trade-offs before you begin. You may even find that partial wins in the right places will have more positive impact than full wins where they won't make as much of a difference. Then have a light enough hand on the reins to go where the organization wants to work, not necessarily where you think it should.

HOW TO KNOW YOU'VE APPLIED THIS LEVER WELL

❑ You have good reasons for starting where you have—and for going where you've gone.

❑ Change pulls you through the organization—you're not trying to push it forward.

❑ At some point along the way, you find yourself surprised about where you're working, with whom, or on what.

❑ More and more, you are working with people who are more and more energized.

❑ You've explored different scenarios and trade-offs along the way.

6

DEVELOP A FUTURE PEOPLE WANT TO CALL THEIR OWN

The question that usually comes up first in any change effort is "What's in it for me?" It's a legitimate question. If you can't answer it in a way that makes sense to those asking, don't bother trying to move forward until you do. What's in it for me to care about the change you are trying to create? How is it going to benefit me? What is it going to cost me? What can I expect in return? Don't assume you know someone else's answer and waste time trying to convince them. Have a conversation. Explore it together. Help others discover what the value could be for them. It's often more powerful for people to answer this for themselves.

A Common Problem: So Many Ask "What's in It for Me?"

This problem has been around since the beginning of organizations. If I decide what I am getting is worth what I am giving, I invest. If I see that equation out of balance, I stay on the sidelines. In small team meetings and large group town halls about change work, this question gets asked early and often. What may make a change worthwhile for one person may be what is unpalatable to another. One person may be motivated by safety and security, another by opportunities for advancement and adventure. Your job is to respond to "What's in it for me?" with integrity and in ways that are compelling enough to engage others in your venture.

Solution: Develop a Future People Want to Call Their Own

The lever Develop a Future People Want to Call Their Own leads people to feel proud of the future they are creating. Each person needs to see the value of a new future for them personally. The goal is to create something that works for the entire organization and each business unit, division, function, team, and individual. It's a tall order, but one worth striving to achieve. This is about getting to the most workable answer for all. It doesn't mean that everyone is going to get everything they want. Reality is unavoidable. Some people's future may not reside with your organization. Treat these people with the same respect and care reserved for those who will be staying. In any case, without a picture of where you're headed that people are excited to claim as their own, you're going to have a tough time getting anywhere.

STORY

We were working with a hospitality company, holding a series of events around the world. The company's purpose for these events was to improve quality and the customers' experience at each property. The focus of this effort was to create a vision of quality for each property. One element of the agenda was for the leaders to solicit feedback from their employees about a draft vision; they would then integrate that feedback overnight and re-present the revised vision to the group the following morning. When the leadership team at one property made their presentation the next morning, they were greeted with silence. Not a word. No clapping. No arguing.

Nothing. We had the table groups turn in and have a conversation about what they thought was happening in the room (an old consultant trick when one can't think of anything else to do!). When we opened the floor again, one person stood up and explained that there was a basic issue that had still gone unaddressed.

This person said, "You don't say hello in the hallways when you pass us." The executives on stage didn't quite understand the issue at first, but the general manager did. These employee "members of the team" didn't feel valued. The GM asked her executive team colleagues one by one whether they would commit to saying hello in the hallways going forward. One by one, they made the commitment, following their boss's cue as to the gravity of the situation. After the last executive committed to saying hello, a man in the back of the room stood up and shouted, "We love you, ma'am!"

What was in it for these people to be greeted in the hallways? To be seen. The issue wasn't with the vision, quality standards, or doing business in new ways. It was much more basic. It was about whether these people would be proud to be part of the future their executive team was asking them to join in creating. What you see as the answer to "What's in it for me?" and what it might be for others could be quite different. Your job is to figure out what it is and find a way to respond to it.

How This Lever Helps Create Faster, Easier, Better Results

The Develop a Future People Want to Call Their Own lever challenges you to find a future and ways to create it that inspire the entire organization. The more people your change works for, the more people will work for your change. By applying this lever, you can achieve faster, easier, better results in your change work, for the following five reasons:

1. *The more that people are excited about the future being created, the more that people will engage in creating it.* There is strength in numbers. The more people supporting the work, the easier it is to accomplish. The more people working *for* you, the fewer working *against* you. When people around you are motivated to create meaningful change, you want to join the crowd. Instead of people sitting around the coffee station

or watercooler and complaining, they gather together to share successes, solve problems, and encourage each other to continue working on change. These conversations create a virtuous cycle.

2. *Alignment around a common, desired future leads to speed.* Futures that meet everyone's needs are futures around which people get aligned. And alignment leads to speed. People have found common ground, firm footing that they can all work from together. When people see a future that is motivating to them, they work in concert to create it. This alignment occurs throughout the organization. It decreases the friction that typically slows change work. Finding a future that works for all means everyone can pull in the same direction and, in doing so, accelerate the pace of change.

3. *Smarter futures result from those that satisfy more stakeholders.* Futures that have to work for multiple parties have been stress-tested by people with different interests. Those that survive this level of analysis have much better odds of standing the test of time. People who care about different aspects of how to meet the customers' needs have weighed in. Other stakeholders' desires have

been accounted for. Competitors' potential moves are considered, as is the workability of the plan to get there. Some questions to explore in setting these criteria:

- Can we make this future real with our current capabilities, or do we need to buy or develop others?
- Is it a future that is going to engage employees or leave them wanting?
- Is it a future that people will want to create?
- Does the future fit with the organization's vision and mission?

Don't rush to judgment. The time you take upstream in crafting this collective future will earn you dividends for a long time to come.

4. *The best of the past and present is part of a strong future.* This reason recalls the polarity work from chapter 1. People are proud of the ways they've worked that have been successful in the past. Yes, some of what has gotten you where you are needs to be left behind, even, at times, when it led to past success. But there are other things from the past that will serve you well in the future. What's crucial is studying and understanding the past and present with a careful eye to what to bring forward. To develop a future that you want to claim as

your own means that you also have to come to terms with your past—the good, the bad, and the ugly.

5. *A future that people want to call their own is a sustainable future.* When you get the future right for everyone, people care about making sure that it is not only achieved but also preserved. Pride in that future taps into a deep well of emotion, one that carries with it a yearning to maintain hard-won progress. You receive no points for short-term wins with no lasting impact. Futures that speak only to some people are short lived if they come into existence at all. The bottom line is that you can't count on gains being sustained over time. Unfortunately, you get what I call Teflon change. The nonstick variety.

STORY

We once held a series of meetings in a consumer products manufacturing company. It used to have a sterling reputation, but had fallen on hard times. Quality was suffering, innovation had become nonexistent, and costs were rising. Complacency had overtaken the operation, and several major customers had already taken their business to competitors. The situation was bleak.

The team planning these events decided that their colleagues needed to hear hard truths if they were to realize that major changes were needed. They reached out to customers who had already placed orders elsewhere and invited them to speak at the events. Customer representatives came and educated people about their business, challenges they were facing, the future they envisioned, and what they needed from suppliers to make that vision a reality. People in the company were humbled by what they heard. They asked questions to better understand their ex-customers' needs. Although it was too late this time around, maybe what they learned would help with their next customer. The events ended, changes were agreed on, plans were made, and commitments to providing a quality product were affirmed. Then something remarkable happened.

The ex-customers who had been at the event called the company's sales team. They wanted to give it another go. On a trial basis. They had been so impressed with the care and concern expressed at the events that they believed the future could be different than the past. This collaboration continued going forward. The consumer products company had won their business back. What had not even been considered possible became a reality. If the ex-customers had been invited to this event with the goal of convincing them to stick around, it likely wouldn't have worked. They'd have seen through the ruse. Instead, they experienced a sincere attempt by the company to do better in the future. In creating a future that members of the company wanted to call their own, they also created one that their former customers wanted to join.

Success Factors in Applying This Lever

Ensure that you end up with a future that people want to call their own by putting the following five success factors in place. Stack the odds in your favor by marking them off one by one.

Factor One: Identify Collaborators for an Ideal Future

The first step in understanding your collaborators' desires is to identify your partners in creation. Once someone thinks they are a member of this team, they just became one. To qualify, they need only have a stake in the work you are doing. It's easier to develop a future that people want to call their own if you keep those crafting it to a minimum. It's also quicker. But easier and quicker are not always better. Think bigger. Sometimes these folks may be obvious to identify. Make a first-draft list. Talk to them. Ask them who else might need to be included in the conversation about your collective future, and invite them too.

Factor Two: Engage Your Stakeholders in Ways They Will Want to Engage with You

Creating this future is not all on you. It can't be. You don't have all the answers. How you ask others to participate can be the difference between welcoming new partners on board or being forced to go it alone. The kind of community you help create with these stakeholders now will foster the kind of relationships you have with them later. Be authentic. Speak your truth and invite them to speak theirs. Do so in ways that welcome them as valuable members of the team, and soon they'll become critical players in a future you all want to call your own.

Factor Three: Persevere: It Will Serve You Well

It's not easy to develop a future that people are proud to call their own. When things get tough, people often protect their own interests more than they try to advance the common good. They say, "Why should I risk working with you when I might do better looking out for only myself?" Don't give up if things get rocky, seem unclear, or aren't working out smoothly. If it were easy, everyone would be creating these kinds of futures. As you feel your patience shorten, step away ... and then reengage. This is also about holding on to your own hopes and dreams. Stand your ground. Your being clear is not the enemy of making things work for all. You are part of that "all." Remember, there's no win in making things work for everyone but you.

Factor Four: Get Creative by Gaining a New Perspective

This is the time for no-holds-barred creativity. You're not going to craft something that works for so many by taking a linear path. This is a tough task. It's hard enough to get a few close colleagues on the same page. How is it possible with people who appear to be in opposition to your goals? Think outside the box. Instead of trying to cut the problem down to size, blow it up as big as you can. Take the opposite point of view from the one you own. Borrow someone else's ideas and try them on for size. Take a step back. Maybe you'll see connections between what different people want that have previously gone unnoticed.

Factor Five: Give Yourself Permission to Get It Wrong

You can get this future-creating business wrong many times. You need to get it right only once. If you miss the mark, try again. Don't get too invested in any one scenario. You're likely to miss a lot more than you make. Shooting percentage doesn't count in this game. Know there will be big bombs and close losses. Don't take things personally. And don't let anyone else do so either. We're aiming for a high standard when we use the Develop a Future That People Want to Call Their Own lever, one you're not going to hit easily. Preserve relationships with key people so that they will want to live to fight another day—together.

STORY

We were asked by a client of ours to engage with a local community. The client wanted to have a collaborative discussion about the impact that its new facilities would have on the community's well-being. This is a typical issue that occurs between development organizations and residents in all sorts of situations. Communities want to keep their natural environment untouched. Growing companies mining natural resources are certain to disturb the intricate ecological balance that has been in existence for years. How do you develop a future that people want to call their own when the underlying interests seem so at odds?

A key element in the fledgling partnership was to establish a council to govern how the two groups would collaborate. When two parties do not trust each other, a process with integrity can bridge the gap. The next thing we did was to have representatives from each group get to know one another as people, not as representatives of their respective groups. They compared notes on families and what they appreciated most about the work they did and lives they lived. This approach of "connection before content" was critical, a lesson I learned from fellow consultants Dick and Emily Axelrod, who first heard it from a leader in the field of organization change, Peter Block.[19] Instead of beginning the process assuming the worst of each other, they began with a foundation of meaningful relationships.

Eventually we got around to the challenging work of finding a way forward that both groups wanted to call their own. The central question became "How can we make this work for everyone?" instead of "How can we ensure that our rights are not violated?" This shift in thinking and approach opened new ideas that set boundaries on the company's environmental impact. The council also made sure the company could conduct a profitable business. New extraction methods were developed that minimized the impact to the surrounding environment. The council weighed in on all important decisions, and no actions were taken by either party until the council had approved a given proposal. As the project progressed, the two groups were able to work in ways that took everyone's interests into account.

How to Know You've Applied This Lever Well

Get the success factors right, and it's time to check your progress. Track how far you've advanced by assessing where you are in your change work against the five dimensions described here.

Shared Commitment Grows over Time

People aren't used to having difficult conversations that end well. The first order of business is typically to be sure they get what they want. They are so busy trying to make sure they are not taken advantage of that working together becomes a long-forgotten afterthought. Standard operating procedures begin with starting on opposite sides of an issue, then collecting information that reinforces your beliefs, and finally repeating this same process again and again. Commitment grows over time in these scenarios. But it's commitment to *my* cause, not *our* cause.

The only way shared commitment works is to have a common future. The energy and excitement people feel when they make this shift are unmistakable. There is less rush to judgment. The trust developed through shared commitment can be counted on when discussions get difficult and disagreements occur. Often the more complex the situation and the longer it takes to find a preferred solution, the greater the commitment each party gains.

"Win-Lose" Language Is Heard Less and Less

A culture change takes place when you begin looking for futures that people want to call their own. You can hear these new dynamics in the conversations people have. There is less defensiveness. Fewer "I" statements and more "We" propositions. When everyone is looking out for everyone's best interests, people can let go of their protectionist worldview. Something surprising shows up. Others begin watching to make sure your needs get met, and you start looking for ways that theirs can be. We're no longer considering a fixed pie where if I win, you have to lose. The game changes. You're no longer looking out for number 1. Everyone is looking out for everybody. The only win is an "all win."

People Are Excited as Success Emerges

There may be nothing more exciting than seeing a future that you are part of, have created, and in which you believe, taking shape. There are plenty of reasons why this is true. You may be working more effectively, personally and organizationally. Perhaps you're energized by more completely fulfilling your personal or organizational potential. You are part of creating a real, live future that you desire. Whether it's your team, organization, community, country, or planet, you are improving the world around you—for yourself and others. Your self-esteem grows as your success expands. It's exciting to see reality begin to change before your eyes. Perhaps nothing is more difficult or rewarding than the act of creation. Enthusiasm expands as the future that is being created comes into sharper focus through the acts of your creating it.

Changes Begin to Be Made before Implementation Formally Begins

There's no need to wait to begin experiencing the benefits of Develop a Future People Want to Call Their Own. Any idea you have can be implemented as soon as you can execute it. This success factor borrows from the wisdom of the Think and Act as If the Future Were Now! lever. What can be done today, in some small or large way, to begin making that future real? People will become impatient in the best way possible. They will yearn to realize a future they will be proud to call their own. They aren't satisfied waiting; instead, they are pushing colleagues and leaders to make changes faster than they thought possible. This rapid form of implementation paves the way for even more positive and productive change to come on its heels.

A New Kind of Teamwork Takes Hold

This new kind of teamwork is one for which you don't need training, special offsites, or organization structure changes. It's the natural result of having a future that people want to call their own. People find ways to work together because it is the best path from where they are to where they want to be. You may have needed to push people to work together before. You no longer need to make a case for change. People naturally see partnering as the best strategy for realizing this future. People now build bridges between silos that previously got in the way. Teams no longer work at cross-purposes. People are willing to try new working arrangements, assess progress, and improve the next time around. When teamwork is getting easier, you'll know you're on the right path with this lever.

Examples of This Lever in Action

The stories here show two different settings and types of changes, but in both cases the changes being made needed to include a broad cross section of stakeholders. Read on and see how each organization tackled the tough work of finding futures that worked for all.

STORY: STRATEGIC PLANNING IN A 150-MEMBER COLLEGE, PART OF A LARGER UNIVERSITY

We were working with a 150-person college on a strategic planning effort. It was very important to the dean that the process be highly participative and that it engage all faculty, staff, and stakeholders. A strategic planning team comprising representatives from all three groups worked over a twelve-month period. The team was in charge of everything from designing the overall effort to supporting the many meetings where the plan was actually developed.

A questionnaire went out to more than three hundred external stakeholders to kick off the effort to assess their experience of working with the college and what they needed to succeed on their own missions. The faculty and staff met in mixed groups for ninety-minute working sessions aimed at defining the college's mission, vision, strategic goals, objectives, key polarities they would need to leverage to succeed, and detailed implementation plans. Meetings were held on a "drop-in" basis so that it was easier for faculty and staff to participate. A total of 80 percent of faculty and staff joined these meetings.

The data collected from stakeholders, faculty, and staff was synthesized, studied, and translated into a strategic plan that was implemented the following year. Smaller changes, such as collaboration gatherings with other colleges of the university, were implemented straight away. All agreed it would have been easier to scale back the data gathering from stakeholders, as the report itself ran more than two hundred pages. But then it would have been much harder to develop a future that people wanted to call their own because everyone's voice would not have been heard. So the questionnaires went out, the meetings were held, and the data came in—a lot of it!

Fewer faculty and staff could have shaped the plan and done a solid job. But 80 percent was the target number for participation. The college's stakeholders were excited by the changes made in their relationships in the first year of implementation. The power of creating this future that people wanted to call their own was felt throughout the system; the dean received positive feedback on the approach and product from all those engaged.

STORY: CREATING PROFESSIONAL DEVELOPMENT CAREER LADDERS IN A FIFTEEN-HUNDRED-PERSON MILITARY TESTING FACILITY

A civilian-based military munitions-testing facility had no history of professional career ladders when we began working with them. People were promoted to fill vacant jobs, but there was no rhyme or reason to how it was done. New hires had no idea how they could progress to more complex, more highly skilled jobs.

A new commanding officer overseeing the facility decided it was time to right the ship. We developed an effort that engaged all fifteen hundred people in the organization in providing input as to what they wanted the development process to do for them. Then a core team, working with the HR lead of the operation and our external team, crafted an entire career development system from scratch. The core team oversaw an effort where new software was implemented. Performance feedback was included as a regular course of business between managers and employees. Broad-based participation led to the creation of both engineering and management career ladders. Then it was time for feedback. What did the members of the organization think of the proposed system?

A series of large group meetings were held to solicit feedback on needed revisions to the draft plans. The finalized plans were implemented successfully, winning an award from a global association charged with evaluating HR systems for the quality and level of engagement in the effort. This change work never would have been possible without acknowledging that the future being created had to be one that people would want to call their own.

People creating a future they want to call their own is a powerful engine for change. There is pride and excitement in bringing a desired future to fruition. It truly is a case where both the journey and the destination are worth experiencing. New relationships forged among stakeholders in the college during the process of developing the strategic plan laid a solid foundation for a collaborative future. The testing facility employees had a double payoff from their work: a future organization to which they wanted to belong and paths to their individual futures they looked forward to achieving.

HOW TO KNOW YOU'VE APPLIED THIS LEVER WELL

☐ Shared commitment grows over time.

❏ "Win-lose" language is heard less and less.

❏ People are excited as success emerges.

❏ Changes begin to be made before implementation formally begins.

❏ A new kind of teamwork takes hold.

7

FIND OPPORTUNITIES FOR PEOPLE TO MAKE A MEANINGFUL DIFFERENCE

People are busy. They're overwhelmed with their regular job, most of which is filled with the same routines day after day. Accountants balance the books. Frontline workers directly serve the customer, or create products that will. HR representatives pay attention to pay, benefits, and meeting employment guidelines. This is important work. It needs to be done, and done well, for an organization to thrive. But the world of change creates unique opportunities, opportunities to make a meaningful difference in creating an organization's future. Identify these opportunities and take advantage of them.

Common Problem: People Get to Do Only the Routine Work of Their Regular Job

People join organizations with a basic social contract. They work and get paid for doing so. In the best organizations, they are treated well, challenged, and given opportunities to learn, grow, and develop. It's a fair deal. But how much impact can one person really have as they do their work day in and day out? Formal leaders have more opportunities for influence than others. Informal leaders have the respect of their peers and often the ear of senior management.

There are those who would argue that doing their job well *is* making a difference. And it is. But that's a different kind of difference. It's one that supports the daily functioning of the enterprise. This is critical work. But I'm talking about a bigger difference. One that holds the promise of changing the trajectory of the individual, team, and organization. There is no more important work than altering the course of your destiny. That is reserved solely for the work of change.

Solution: Find Opportunities for People to Make a Meaningful Difference

The work of Leverage Change comes with new rules. We are no longer talking about doing what we have always done. It's time to begin exploring new, different, and even better ways of working that offer ready opportunities for people to make their mark. Look for ways to engage others in the meaningful tasks of building a new and better future. Change can be overwhelming for some. They can feel as though they're losing control. The future can be an unpredictable place ... unless you're in the thick of creating it.

In those cases, people trade their fears of the unknown for the excitement of being part of something larger than themselves. There are all sorts of opportunities to make a difference in change efforts founded on participative principles. Changes made by the many for the many give people a chance to make their most valuable contributions. These contributions offer ingenuity to the entire organization with the goal of enhancing the lives and performance of colleagues, customers, suppliers, and other stakeholders.

STORY

Another example of Applying One Lever occurred in the case of a manufacturing client of ours. There was no formal change program in place or developed as part of this work. We looked for an opportunity for people to make a meaningful difference, and the lever and the people in the organization did the rest of the work.

The engineering staff was seen to be aloof, above the fray of everyday conflicts that plagued the rest of the business. We had the engineers visit their internal customers, asking how they could best support them in the work they needed to do. A simple question ... followed by an avalanche of good ideas. People from the manufacturing arm of the organization explained how important it would be to them to be involved earlier in design conversations to help assess how difficult it would be to manufacture what was being designed. This input was just the ticket for the engineers to realize the difference they could make for their manufacturing counterparts. These newfound change agents seized this opportunity. They invited their new partners into design concept meetings, including their ideas in the earliest prototypes.

Look for an opening for others to make a difference, large or small. Be prepared to be surprised by the groundswell of support that awaits your request. Just like those engineers, people are looking for ways to contribute in your organization.

How This Lever Helps Create Faster, Easier, Better Results

The Find Opportunities for People to Make a Meaningful Difference lever encourages you to be open to people playing new roles in change work. People aren't just asked to do work because it needs to be done. The work has to be reframed to focus on how it makes a difference in the larger scheme of things. When those in the organization see themselves making a difference in their work, you'll find differences in the work the organization does. Your change work will become more effective when you and others find these opportunities for more and more members of your organization. Here are five reasons why:

1. *People step up in a whole new way when asked to take on big work. Big work, important work, matters to an organization's future. It also matters to those doing it. Work that makes a difference demands*

extra attention. And extra attention results in higher-quality work. This becomes a cycle that feeds on itself. Higher-quality work increases the likelihood that the desired difference will be made. Stack the odds in your favor. Trust people to do critical work, support them as needed, and reward them for doing it well.

2. *You can vary the roles of senior leaders depending on the situation.* This lever does not apply only to those lower in the hierarchy. When it comes to making a difference in change work, there is an entire continuum of options for the role of those at the top, from making all the calls to making none of them. These are the extremes. In most cases, you'll find yourself somewhere between the two. It's important to know that this continuum exists and is available to you and others in your organization. As in the technology company example in the next story, leaders can play a very strong role of direction early in the process when setting strategy, then reverse things 180 degrees when it comes time for implementation. This flexibility ensures that meaningful roles can be found for all people engaged in change work.

3. *Each task and role is clear so that there are no misunderstandings.* When you focus on finding opportunities for people to make a difference, you will make clearer requests. Problems surface when people think they have a say in a decision but in fact have only been asked for input. Misunderstandings like these undermine trust. People think one thing, find out another, and feel tricked. You need to be clear up front about when, where, why, and how people will be making a difference in change work. This doesn't mean that everyone will always be happy with the decisions you've made. You must be certain, though, that everyone understands what is being asked of them and how it contributes to the success of your effort.

4. *The right people do the right work.* The work that needs to be done and who can best do it are unique to each change effort. Start with the work. Sometimes you'll need a larger group to do the work justice. At other times, a small, tight circle will serve you better. Ask yourself these questions:

   • Who has the information, expertise, and experience to best do this work?

- Who needs to be engaged so that implementation issues are raised and resolved early in the process?

- Are there people who will see opportunities or traps that others might be prone to miss?

- Whose support are you going to need down the line to ensure that changes made last a long time?

When you answer these questions wisely, you'll be creating a team that together can make the difference needed for you to succeed.

5. *People will help recruit others to join the team.* It's a privilege to make a contribution to the greater good. People will welcome being asked to work on needed changes and make a difference. Be clear about why they are uniquely needed for you to achieve your goals. Help them see the value they can add, and have them supplement that list based on their own insights. The larger the number of committed members of your team, the higher the likelihood that you will enjoy success. When there are opportunities to make a difference, invitations to join the cause will readily be shared between friends and colleagues.

STORY

We worked with a technology company where profits were down, competition was up, and new technologies were taking hold in the industry. The senior team made the important calls in setting the business strategy. The leaders went about developing a complex, scenario-based strategy that accounted for a range of pricing changes in the marketplace. Mergers and acquisitions were on the table, as were schemes to go it alone.

Strategy sessions were closed-door meetings, with regular updates shared with the entire company. Others in the organization didn't mind missing these grueling fact-finding missions. They were asked up front to say when they thought it made sense to join the change effort. The answer? To be kept updated on progress as it was made and to take charge when it came time for implementation. Implementation is where prior efforts had fallen short. The meaningful difference that needed to be made this time for success to be ensured resided in this arena. When implementation time arrived, the leaders went straight into "servant leader" mode. People from across the organization were now in charge of implementation efforts. Executives assumed the role of supporting them in translating strategy into action—and ultimately, results. Supervisors and their teams requested specific support from different members of the leadership team. The leaders did their best to respond, embracing their new role of supporting the entire organization. Profits increased in year 1. It was a situation where leaders and others in the company made unique differences, each required to achieve faster, easier, better results.

Success Factors in Applying This Lever

Challenge the belief that those at the top of the house have the greatest chance to make a difference in change work. What's most important is to ensure that each person in your organization has their best opportunity to make a meaningful difference. When you put the following success factors in place, you can be confident that members of your business can make that unique contribution.

Factor One: Find the Best Way for People to Make a Difference in Your Organization

Leaders and organizations have their own ways of best engaging people meaningfully in change work. The reasons for these preferences can be sorted into one or more of the following three groups: past practice (This is the way we've always done things around here); current competence (We know how to do things this way); future success (This will be the easiest way to get the job done). All good reasons to consider. However, a great way for people to experience making a difference in your change work is an important one missing from the list: what people in your organization experience as the best way for them to make a profound difference in change work.

Factor Two: Gain Agreement from Key Stakeholders about Who Decides What, and the Difference That Can Make

The when, what, and how of change work are not decisions for you to make alone. What other players think counts. They will give you wise counsel from which to arrive at your decisions. How you choose who makes a decision can be as important as what you decide. Patterns you establish now set expectations for the future. Not all stakeholders may agree with one another on how to best collaborate at any point in time. Try having them talk to one another about their desires and concerns. They often don't know what others are thinking about control and influence. Having the conversation itself is a form of making a difference in the bigger picture, and that's a solid start. You may also be surprised. Asking people what they want may lead to answers that are different than you expected. You'll never know if you don't ask.

Factor Three: Discover New Ways to Involve People

Be open to any way to involve people that provides an opportunity to make a significant difference. Direction and participation give you two choices about how to allocate power and influence. Find creative ways to combine the two. Don't be afraid to go to the extremes at any point. It is about balancing the needs of these two dynamics over time. Sometimes you may be focused only on direction, other times on participation. Think unconventionally. Typically, steering groups tasked with setting direction for change efforts are made up of senior executives. Implementation task forces tend to be staffed by people closest to frontline work. Ask people if this is the right approach for your organization. Think about turning the logic for both these groups upside down. Have frontline workers represented in your steering groups, and executives serving on your implementation teams. They'll bring fresh perspectives, naïve questions, and insights that otherwise would be missed if you stick with traditional approaches.

Factor Four: Worry Less about Having What You Say Count

You have your opinions about when and how to involve people in your change effort, even about what qualifies as making a difference. What decisions do others care about making? Everyone in the organization is interested in having what they say matter. Take one person out of that equation, at least for a while. You. Your job is to make sure good decisions are made. You should be focused on ensuring effective collaboration. There will be enough tough challenges to tackle in your change work. Don't become one of the challenges that others have to deal with. If important points haven't found their way into a conversation, make sure they do. Take a firm stand if you think you must. But if you become overinvested, to the point that you need to be right regardless of what others are saying, your caring and commitment have gone too far.

Factor Five: Get People Focused on Making a Difference for Everyone

People have individual agendas when it comes to organizations and change. That's called being human. We've already covered the "What's in it for me?" world of concerns. Another critical question to ask is "Will their participation make a difference for others and the work?" Imagine the commitment you'll gain from people knowing that what matters to them matters to the organization as well. You need to help people make connections between the work they are doing and the organization's larger objectives. Make these connections easy for people to see.

STORY

Theaters often have "Talk Back" sessions following a play's performance. It's a chance for the audience to ask questions of the actors, the director, and even the playwright to better understand what they've seen. They pose all kinds of questions, about everything from costumes to characters. Patrons become participants, not just observers. Knowing that customers like to be involved in the theater's operations, we took advantage of that opportunity.

What contribution is more profound than shaping the future direction of the enterprise? Using a takeoff of the Talk Back approach, we once held "Talk Forward" sessions with audiences of a community theater. The idea was to capture ideas for the theater's future. There was no decision-making done at these sessions. It was a creative way, in line with the theater's culture, of engaging its audience in shaping the theater's direction. Whom to involve and how doesn't pertain just to members of the organization. Customers count, too. The theater received input that audiences wanted to see more foreign productions, even if the plays were subtitled and performed in their original language. You are the one who draws the line around people invited to make a difference in your change work. Make it as big a circle as you please.

How to Know You've Applied This Lever Well

Get the five success factors in place and then test how well you've done. Prove your success in applying this lever to yourself and your situation, seeing how many check marks you get from the list at the end of the chapter.

Over Time, You Experience Less Resistance about Who Decides What

If you're building alignment as you go, you'll feel more momentum as you move forward. You'll benefit from people's greater trust and confidence in the work. Early on, you may have had to resort to asking people to "trust the process." Now they have influence over their involvement as proof that your work has integrity and that their contributions make a real difference. They may not like all the decisions being made in the effort, but they can count on the approach being fair and based on objective criteria. You'll be better able to appreciate what others are willing to let go of in order to hold on to something that they value more.

People Embrace the Work They Are Doing

When people engage in work that is meaningful, they look forward to the work they need to be doing. It's the right work for them. They have been or will be motivated to develop the knowledge, skills, and abilities to do it well, and they're proud to lend a helping hand. When there is a need for partnering, people reach out and ask for help, and it's willingly offered. Check-ins don't feel like checkups to make sure the work is being done right. Seek help, and volunteers' hands rise into the air. You're not stuck with the silent treatment, people casting their eyes down hoping not to get called on, as though you are in your sophomore chemistry class in high school. Special task forces are set up quickly and easily. Your change work works well.

People Realize Their Full Potential

When people are able to make a difference in change work, each person can make their most valuable contribution. What happens when the organization doesn't have the competencies required by the change work that needs to be done? People learn. Others are invited to join the cause. They are asked to do more than they themselves believe might be possible. For the good of the organization, they raise their game, sometimes even surprising themselves and others by developing new capabilities. People are challenged to stretch themselves, grow, and develop through their change work.

People Are Valued for the Work They Are Doing

People are asked to do work that matters, whether it's leading or following. Others take note of the contributions you are making, and you are valued for doing your work well. It's work that is important for the organization's future, and it is appreciated by many. It's easy to catch people doing something right and to say something affirming about it. Good stories abound. People let each other know when their work makes someone else's job easier. Whether it's expressed by internal or external customers, the feeling of appreciation is the same. What you do matters to many. Succeeding in your work makes it easier for everyone to feel better about their contributions.

Work Is Getting Done Well

Work done well is the surest sign that you are on the right path to enabling people to make a meaningful difference in change work. You have high quality. Tasks are completed on time and within budget. Handoffs are clear and made seamlessly between groups. The subjective data—how people feel about the work getting done—is just as solid. There is broad-based agreement that the right work is being done. You've struck the right balance of contributions. When information is needed, it's available. When people are needed to do work, they are eager to begin. When there are important questions that need to be answered, healthy conversations ensue. The right people are around the table, and people not around the table don't mind that they're not there. Those participating look to formal or informal leaders, design teams, and task forces to get direction. Success is what matters more than anything else.

Examples of This Lever in Action

Two very different change efforts are described here; both needed broad-based involvement to succeed. Read the stories and learn how people were afforded opportunities to contribute in significant ways needed for change work to be effective.

STORY: STRENGTHENING CITIZEN–POLICE RELATIONSHIPS—EVERYBODY MAKING A PROFOUND DIFFERENCE

We have worked with local police, government, and many other stakeholders in several cities across the US. It's been challenging and, no question, important work to be done. Everybody involved has had an opportunity to make a difference and has known that the projects could not have progressed without their participation. The goal of these efforts has been to further strengthen citizen–police relationships grounded in trust and legitimacy. The heartbeat of these projects has been a series of dialogues between citizens and police. These facilitated conversations were called "action sessions" to emphasize that the meetings were about more than just talk. Gatherings lasted ninety minutes and were focused on leveraging the polarity between public safety and public trust. Public safety was defined as the combination of effective policing, government services, and resident involvement that creates a safe, secure, and livable city.

Public trust referred to a deep belief that police officers, those in government services, and residents will treat each other with fairness, equity, dignity, and respect, and will act in the interest of one another's and the collective well-being.

Action sessions included an explanation of the project, a listing of diverse project sponsors, and citizens and police officers having honest, open discussions. They explored their current perceptions of the relationship, and the actions that could be taken by each group that would enhance their connection.

Implementation of ideas began even before all the action sessions had been completed. Large, complex policy-oriented changes were acted on, such as community policing objectives laid out in a Presidential Task Force for Police Accountability report. Simple yet high-impact steps were also taken. For example, once a month the police garage in one community opens, and people are invited to bring in their cars for taillight replacement and other minor repairs for free. (Otherwise, such infractions would result in tickets.) In this same community, ten of the eighty-six actions defined in the three-year plan were implemented before the plan was even completed.

People making big differences were key to the success of this effort. The project management team of police, city government representatives, and leaders from a local university conducting research on the work set parameters and managed the effort. A cross section of the entire community was asked to be involved through a steering group to oversee the process. That group decided to invite one hundred citizens to join a community influencers group who would engage others in attending the sessions. Thirty facilitators were recruited in the community to join the cause, leading small groups through their conversations. Clear lines of authority and role descriptions were defined up front. This type of large-scale effort required participation at many levels and coordination between project teams and external stakeholders, such as leaders of the faith communities. Finding opportunities for people to make a meaningful difference was essential to the success of these projects.

STORY: ACTION-LEARNING PROJECTS IN A GLOBAL SAFETY-TESTING BUSINESS

As part of an executive development series on strategy and paradox, we brought together thirty leaders from different business units for an action-learning session. Originally held for one team, the experience was requested by eleven other groups in the company, despite having no budget allocated for it and no internal marketing campaign. They asked to participate all on their own. The opportunity to make a meaningful difference through the program—and the positive reviews heard on the grapevine—led to more and more of the sessions being held.

The groups spent three days together working through business strategy and paradoxes they experienced in leading their businesses. The paradoxes, areas that mattered for the participants and the company to thrive in the future, were identified by the participants themselves through pre-session questionnaires. Participants then worked in groups based on having identified similar paradoxes before the gathering. For example, paradoxes analyzed included "investing in growth and meeting execution goals." Another one addressed was "getting my work done and learning and developing my leadership competencies."

Subgroups identified business issues related to each paradox. The subgroups then set up action-learning projects with critical success factors, resourcing requirements, and implementation plans. These were all areas in which the subgroups had accountabilities, and it made sense for them to lead. Subgroups also had input to one another's work because the issues they were addressing were experienced by the entire business unit—another opportunity to make a meaningful difference through supporting their colleagues.

Formal leaders of each business unit reviewed plans and provided additional input. Participants then tested plans they'd developed with others in the organization. The work needed to make a meaningful difference for everyone, not just those attending the sessions.

Nothing is mundane about the business of change. There are many opportunities for people to make contributions to creating their collective future. Take the task of finding these opportunities seriously. Provide a welcome invitation for people to become full-fledged members of your change team. Every time you make a decision that affects others, try to find ways for them to contribute. This may be in making the actual decision, but doesn't have to be. Gathering data, exploring options, and weighing trade-offs are all ways to become involved in change work and, in doing so, make important, meaningful contributions.

HOW TO KNOW YOU'VE APPLIED THIS LEVER WELL

❏ Over time, you experience less resistance about who decides what.

❏ People embrace the work they are doing.

❏ People's full potential is realized.

❏ People are valued for the work they are doing.

❏ The work is getting done well.

8

MAKE CHANGE WORK PART OF DAILY WORK

People complain about having too much on their plate. Now you want to add change efforts to an already long list of daily to-dos? What if we flipped that belief? What if change work was also part of daily work? Don't deal with change only through specially designed offsite meetings. Change work can also become one and the same as daily work. It's on everyone's agenda, every day. Daily work has been part of organizations since day 1. Why struggle with the sustainability of change when you can link it to the most enduring aspect of every organization?

Common Problem: People's Plates Are Already Full

"What else do they expect of me? I'm already doing the best I can." "The latest restructuring is just another name for putting more work on my plate." "Do more with less."

"Work smarter, not harder." Many people are working longer hours and taking work home with them every day, and weekends too, and feel as though they've never left the office. All organizations struggle with this issue. Big system-wide changes require special resources and teams. But what if there were a way to create needed improvements in your organization by putting change work and daily work together in ways that made sense and life became easier, not more difficult?

> The Make Change Work Part of Daily Work lever is special. Of all eight, it is the lever that, when applied, is always done as Applying One Lever. It's inherent in its design. The Applying-One-Lever approach brings about organization change without the need for a formal program. Because this lever is about expanding how you define your daily work to include change work, you'll never need to design and implement a formal program to use it. The descriptions and stories that follow show you ways and places you can use this lever to gain positive impact from it all on its own.

Solution: Make Change Work Part of Daily Work

Take a journey on the road less traveled. What about all those changes you can make without needing a formal program to support them? That's what this lever is all about. Create a new reality. One you want to—and can—live in. This lever is as much about your mindset as it is about your behavior. Change one and you'll change the other. Part of this approach is a variation on what the Japanese call *kaizen*, "improvement." Everyone from the CEO to frontline workers makes small improvements on a continuous basis. Small improvements add up to big changes.

When you find ways to make change part of your daily routine, you'll get better at finding new and more effective ways to do business. Look for opportunities every day to make the organization's work more successful. Make it a point to share best practices so that other parts of the business don't have to struggle with problems you've already solved. Focus on improving your team's performance in every meeting you hold. Ask a colleague well versed in the task you're tackling to coach you in completing a job well done.

You can't apply this lever to every organization change you're undertaking. There are aspects of big projects that don't neatly fit into your average day, major shifts that will require above-and-beyond effort through formal projects. But the more you find ways to apply this lever, the more leverage you'll gain from it.

STORY

Executives of an entertainment company needed to change how they worked together. This change wasn't going to be accomplished in just one offsite team-building session. They knew they needed an entire overhaul of their operating system:

- How they made decisions
- How work was done between meetings
- How they held themselves and one another accountable for commitments they had made

They hadn't been ineffective in the past. The work got done. It was just demotivating for the team. People showed up for meetings, at least in body if not in spirit. The gatherings were on no one's list of top ten things to do every quarter. The team leader knew she had to make changes, for her own sake as much as for others'. Things were getting painful. Painfully obvious.

So they began their change work, but not with a special announcement or formal program. There were no readiness assessments, task forces, or tiger teams. The leader did, however, set the team up for success in tackling the first issue—how they made decisions—by doing the following:

• Having conversations with each member of the team about her expectations before kicking off the "effort"

• Laying out some guidelines for the first team talk

• Setting time aside in the weekly meeting agenda to address the first topic

• Following through personally to ensure that commitments were completed for interim work that was assigned after the first conversation

Decision-making processes then became another agenda item for standard meetings, not unlike the company's financial reporting. The team explored why balls had been dropped in the past and what impact these missed opportunities had on the business. Everyone agreed that one more attempt of agreeing around the table was not going to do the trick.

Each person received feedback on how the rest of the team viewed their decision-making performance. Using that feedback, they identified the unique issues getting in the way of their functioning. They shared what they believed were the root causes that were causing their shortfalls in this area and what they were going to do to up their game to "exceptional" from their current level. During each subsequent meeting, sixty minutes were devoted to the follow-up issue.

Twice-yearly assessments were conducted. One year later, feedback had improved substantially. Team members' behavior had shifted. No special change effort was ever launched to deal with the situation. The change work was embedded into the daily work of the team.

How This Lever Helps Create Faster, Easier, Better Results

The Make Change Work Part of Daily Work lever takes a fresh look at the age-old problem of people being too busy with their daily work. When everyone's too busy with their regular to-do lists, there's no one left to do the change work. Reframe this showstopper so that anyone can take on every change challenge. With this lever, you can achieve faster, easier, better results in your change work for the following five reasons:

1. *Everybody is working on change every day.* You're trading having a portion of your organization working on change part of the time for having your entire organization working on change all of the time. People see more opportunities to make improvements in how the organization functions because you have more people looking for those improvements more of the time. More changes get made by more people when everyone is working on change every day.

2. *Resistance decreases when everyone is on the change team.* There's no one left out with this approach; no voice goes unheard. The team becomes larger and more powerful. All members of the team are valued. You are no longer dealing with representatives of different stakeholder groups. As people have greater influence and control over changes, resistance diminishes. When they themselves are the ones making these changes, the dynamics shift. They now are part of shaping, directing, and making things

happen in ways that work best for them and their colleagues.

3. *Implementation is more effective.* More people focused on change means more people focused on the implementation of change. That leads to more effective implementation. People know what to do, how to do it, when to do it, and why. They become as well versed in metrics for successful change as they are in metrics for successful business operations. They are as smart and aligned around any change—be it strategy, culture, business processes, or anything else—as they are going about their day job.

4. *People have more and better information on which to base change decisions.* Because everyone is talking about change work occurring every day everywhere, change data is current and accurate. There is zero lag time in reporting progress with change work, as it's shared at the end of each day and the end of each shift, similar to quality and other production numbers in a manufacturing operation. The same goes for lessons learned. Because of this, people are smarter about changes that need to be made and how they can be made most effectively. All change is part of an integrated experience called "work."

5. *Innovation becomes a way of life.* When you make change work part of daily work, improvement ideas become part of daily conversations. Whenever two or more people are gathered, you may hear new ideas to enhance processes and practices. Everyone is invited to contribute, all the time. The day job still gets done, but with a unique twist. It's never separated far from exploring changes that would get that same day job done better than before. Is yesterday's approach to work still good enough for today, or can it be better? That question gets asked and answered often when change work becomes part of daily work.

Success Factors in Applying This Lever

Ensure that you have the following five factors in place, and you've set yourself up to gain the advantages available from this lever.

Factor One: See Change as Everybody's Job

If you don't get buy-in on this factor, you will have failed very early on in your efforts. It's the core of the entire lever. You can't assume that change is someone else's business. It's everyone's responsibility. It needs to be included in everyone's job description and in all team charters. New hires need to understand the kind of organization they're joining. People have to first define for themselves the kinds of changes they believe they can best make. Then they need to gain agreement with their colleagues and whom they report to so that they can define their span of control. Just as alignment in goals is required, alignment in roles is necessary for this lever to be optimized.

Factor Two: Coordinate around Common Goals

When people are making changes on many fronts at once, it's essential that improvements are aligned around common goals. Imagine the mischief created with multiple changes made simultaneously, but working at cross-purposes. First, proposed strategies need to position the organization for winning now and into the future. Second, people need to understand the goals. If people don't understand them, they are left to wonder why they're doing what they're doing. This is confusing at best and demotivating at worst. Third, people have to have confidence in the goals. They need to believe that the goals will get them where they need to go.

Factor Three: Define Clear Measures of Success

If you don't know when you've achieved your goals, you'll be stuck working away at them forever. Getting really good at doing something that's no longer needed is no way to spend precious resources. Because you will be making all sorts of changes, you need to be crystal clear as an entire organization on the unwavering targets at which you are all aiming.

Factor Four: Ensure Everyone Has the Freedom to Make Needed Changes

At first, this factor sounds like a recipe for chaos, and it would be if you didn't have broad-based and deeply understood alignment around goals. This is your fail-safe switch to ensure that the permission granted in this factor is exercised responsibly. You need to be fully committed to this success factor to fully take advantage of this lever. If you're going to take people's freedom away partway through, it's better that you had never given it in the first place.

Factor Five: Be Certain You Are Capable of Making Needed Changes

You win no points for recognizing value-added improvements if they remain only ideas in your mind and not actions in the real world. It doesn't matter whether you make the change yourself or hand it off to someone else who can. You may find that you need upskilling to get the job done. Perhaps you need a team brought together with a wide range of competencies to complete the task. Resources of another type might be your key to success. Time, money, or prioritizing the task higher could be your answer. If you can't make the change with the resources and people in your organization, bring in new people. Partner with specialists to provide the missing link in your chain. Whatever's needed, you need to find a way to get it done. Then do it!

STORY

An entire supervisory group from a medical products company spent one week learning a tool kit for change called How to Manage and Lead Strategically. They were asked to poll their teams before they came so that they had a real business issue to work with in the session. The supervisors applied what they had learned to these change projects with solid success in the session. The plan from there was to have these supervisors learn the tools and return to their work groups, share what they had learned, and incorporate new approaches to change into their regular staff meetings.

The applications proved helpful on a whole range of issues, everything from how to backfill positions caused by a team member's extended time off the job to learning new IT systems while not losing operational uptime. This transformed a change tool into a technique that could be used equally well for achieving faster, easier, better results in any work they did. This is an example of the third application of the levers: Improving Their Own Work through applying the tool. By making change work part of daily work, the supervisors achieved faster, easier, better results in a number of ways. There was no formal change program launched to support their work. But the real value came when the teams began to use the tools on a just-in-time basis. Learning improvement tools—and using them consistently as part of daily work—is one way to bring this lever alive.

How to Know You've Applied This Lever Well

Check yourself against the items described here and the list at the end of the chapter. Make sure you've gotten the best this lever has to offer. Do this well, and it's time to decide if you need to apply another lever in your quest for faster, easier, better results.

Change Is No Longer Thought of as Something Special

Change work has been seen as an unnatural act in organizations for too long. There are special offices set up to manage it. Communications departments take charge of developing change messaging, themes, and slogans. It's time to take back the sole charge of change from specialists. You'll know you have this lever under control when you see that people view changes that they themselves can make as nothing more than their regular work.

It's Hard for People to Distinguish between "Change Work" and "Daily Work"

Interrupt someone midtask in the organization. Ask them whether they're doing change work or daily work. Often, they will either look at you quizzically or respond "Both." Either is an acceptable answer. The key is to collapse the difference between the two. People describe their work in And terms instead of seeing change work and daily work as an Or choice. Some will understand this integration sooner. Others may take longer. Eventually, you can recruit the entire organization. When you've accomplished that, you'll reap the full rewards of this lever.

Change Work Becomes Sustained Work

Lasting change is the holy grail for every organization. The secret to achieving it? Doing change work as sustained work. It's not something that starts and ends. Sustained change can be seen as an oxymoron. Think of it as continuous improvement on steroids—everyone improving the whole system all the time. As you approach the deliverables you originally identified, move these results further toward even greater success. Claim wins along the way. Celebrate progress. Acknowledge when former goals have been achieved and new goals set. Have people understand that the game has changed. It's no longer about reaching the finish line. It's about covering more and more ground.

Every Team Becomes a Change Team

Change is no longer solely the province of specially selected people. No one is rewarded (or sometimes seen to be punished) by being named to a change team. Every member of every team becomes a member of the change team. Securing needed changes of one type or another becomes a major area of responsibility for everyone. Is there a way we can improve our performance? If we were to do business in a different way, could it support our colleagues in another part of the operation in making sustained gains? Adopt constant vigilance for improvement every day, and you'll have mastered this lever.

Your Organization Becomes More "Change-Able"

The more you practice something, the easier it gets. When change becomes part of everyone's full-time job, your organization's skills and abilities in that area will improve.

- You'll learn shortcuts, areas in which you excel, and those where you need an extra push.
- People on teams will naturally gravitate to places where they can add the most value in making improvements.
- Changes will take less time to complete successfully.
- You'll become more effective in making changes you set out to accomplish.
- People across the organization will be working on these improvements continuously.
- Momentum and motivation will feed on each other in a virtuous cycle.

Being a change-able organization may be the greatest competitive advantage that exists. Changing faster, more easily, and better than other players in your market means you will respond faster to innovations and emerging customer needs. You'll be working this muscle on a daily basis. A stronger organization is your reward.

Examples of This Lever in Action

A county government and a large health care provider were each looking for ways to apply this lever to its change work. These are stories of how you too can make change work part of daily work.

STORY: A COUNTY GOVERNMENT LEARNS TO MAKE CHANGE WORK PART OF DAILY WORK

We worked with a county government that served a population of five hundred thousand. It provided everything from park maintenance to enforcing land zoning regulations. Everyone in the organization was invited to be a change agent, to look at their work through a dual lens of change work and daily work.

The county manager spent time with people explaining that they were meant to define this change for themselves. Neither he nor his team was going to be telling them to do anything different. The rest was up to the members of the organization. It was viewed as a grand experiment. No one could predict how

---

the work would progress. One story stands out from the county that demonstrates the power and possibilities of this lever.

There had been conflict for some time between two groups that used a local park. It revolved around when the grass was cut. If it was done in the morning, the wet grass would make a mess on shoes of runners who used the park for training. Do it in the afternoon, and it provided a poor environment for parents pushing strollers trying to calm their babies. The grounds crew, stuck in the middle, tried to arrange their schedule to appease everyone, but somehow, someone always had a complaint. With the added freedom and invitation to be change agents, the grounds crew decided to proactively take the problem into their own hands.

Previously they had felt like a punching bag between the two groups. Now they called a meeting of all interested and affected stakeholders. They put the word out and met one evening; everyone shared their frustrations, including the grounds crew. This was no official change program, just the grounds crew making change work part of their daily work. Interested and affected parties gathered informally for a short conversation. The three groups wanted to find a solution that worked for everyone. The grounds crew asked the runners and parents for ideas on how to resolve the conflict. Together, all three groups mapped out a workable solution. Runners would finish their routines by 10a.m. Parents wouldn't start their walks until 2p.m. Lawn mowing was done during the "down time." Clean shoes for the runners. Quiet strolls for the parents and their babies. A big headache resolved for the maintenance crew. Change work becomes everyone's job when it becomes part of daily work.

STORY: IMPLEMENTING A PATIENT-CENTERED-CARE MODE OF PRACTICE IN A FIFTY-THOUSAND-MEMBER HEALTH CARE ORGANIZATION

The needed change was clear and involved everyone in the organization: implement a patient-centered-care mode of practice in every hospital, ambulatory care center, testing facility, and doctor's office. But how to go about making such a massive transformation? That was another question entirely.

Leaders invited employees across the system to make change work part of their daily work. In short, the leaders unleashed the energy and creativity of their people to make this transformation. People's lives hung in the balance. Coordinated changes based on the latest research were the only way to go. It felt as though there were few degrees of freedom. This was not about independent changes being made by individuals as they saw fit. That would be a disaster. Every application of a lever is unique to the situation to which it is applied.

The process began with an address from the CEO. He spelled out the new role for everyone in the system. They were all in charge of making needed changes. Time was spent ensuring that everyone from the top surgeons to the custodial crews was aligned around what success looked like and how it would be measured. Everything from treatment protocols to business practices was included. The entire organization's culture needed a major overhaul. There was plenty of work for everyone. The typical approach was to gather a manageable group of representatives from across different parts of the organization, have them report to the senior executives on a regular basis, and design the needed changes. Then a rollout to the entire system would come as part of a major change program. Making change work part of daily work suggested another path.

It meant including making change part of everyone's job. How do you do this in a fifty-thousand-member institution? Start with the intention. Then look for all the ways to back up that intention with action. There were special teams set up to take on major projects. However, whenever possible, the teams handed off tasks to regular work teams to advance as part of their "day job." All told, five thousand people in the organization were directly involved in managing and leading this transformation, integrating as many of the changes as possible into the daily work of the institution. Then the implementation team of fifty thousand got to work, integrating as part of normal operations as many of these new ways of working as possible. Innovations in practices and procedures were introduced in regular staff meetings. Implementation began during the teams' next shift. The more that change work became part of daily work, the more successful the effort became.

When perfect isn't possible, take the next best thing. Invite as many people as you can to make change work part of daily work. As I've said before, the more you are able to apply a lever, the greater the leverage you gain from it.

As I noted at the beginning of the chapter, not every change is tailor-made for this lever. Even in the case of the health care system, there were elements of a formal change program needed. But the essence of this lever, that organization-wide changes can sometimes be best married with daily work, is a powerful paradigm. People who have applied this lever report a different mindset and experience than the norm. Creating better ways of doing business doesn't have to feel as much like another task on an already too long to-do list. It's all in a day's work.

HOW TO KNOW YOU'VE APPLIED THIS LEVER WELL

❏ Change is no longer thought of as something special.

> ❑ It's hard for people to distinguish between "change work" and "daily work."
> ❑ Change work becomes sustained work.
> ❑ Every team becomes a change team.
> ❑ Your organization becomes more "change-able."

9

THE POWER AND POSSIBILITIES OF LEVERAGE CHANGE

Leverage Change (n.). A flexible approach that applies eight ways for individuals, teams, and organizations to change that achieves faster, easier, and better results than believed possible.

How do you accelerate the pace of change, lighten your load, and improve your odds of success, all at the same time?

Leverage Change.

Remember from Archimedes that leverage is the compounding force gained by the use of a lever rotating on a fulcrum. It provides an alternative to raw manpower. Translate the Archimedes story to the world of organization change and you're working inside the Leverage Change paradigm, a world of 8 Levers, each tried and tested successfully in addressing a different common problem with change work.

Gaining Great Leverage

This book has been written to give you guidance about how to achieve faster, easier, better results. It's not focused on helping you decide what results will lead to your success. Is innovation going to be the key to winning in your industry in the future? What about expanding your footprint? Maybe there are technology solutions that will make the difference for you and your organization. These are the kinds of decisions on your plate.

At the same time, this topic of what results to achieve is too important to ignore. Faster, easier, better versions of poor, confusing results are a bad answer. The rest of this chapter outlines key points to consider so that you define clear and correct results needed by your organization.

Benefits of Getting Your Results Right

There are five benefits you'll enjoy when you get your desired results right for your organization. Do the work, know where you're headed, and enjoy the products of your work.

1. *Most important, the results you're aiming for enable you to achieve success based on measures that matter to you.* How you define

success is up to you. Maybe it's better teamwork, reduced time to market, or more innovative product design. You decide. Begin where you are now. Understand what's happening around you. Know what you do well. Own what you need to do better. Then set your targets based on what you learn.

2. *Your results provide a rallying point around which to align.* Clear results put a stake in the ground. They're the center point around which everything else organizes. It's hard to get excited about a fuzzy future. Maybe it looks like this. Maybe a little like that. Good luck trying to gain momentum aiming at an uncertain future. Make your results crystal clear, and people will coordinate their efforts and move into the future together.

3. *Right results will tell you when you're on course and off, and what corrections are needed.* The first question to ask is, Are you doing what you said you'd do? Are you following your plans? A second question, sometimes ignored, is, By following the plan, are you achieving the results you desire? If yes, why? If no, why not? Change isn't about moving in a straight line from point A to point B. Assess the impact of actions you're taking.

Use what you learn to determine your next best steps.

4. *You're clear about when you have achieved success.* This is not to be underestimated. Some people keep toiling away long after victory should have been declared. Know when you're done. Without this knowledge, people feel as though they are constantly on a hamster wheel, with no hope of ever getting off. Make a point of finishing—at least with this effort, or a phase of it. Highlight progress made. Set time aside for lessons learned. Then agree on your next goals.

5. *You'll be smarter about how to allocate resources.* Every organization has limited resources. Time, money, energy, and talent invested in change aren't available for other work. When your results are spot-on, conversations about which resources to allocate where become clearer. Have these dialogues, and you can confidently make these decisions knowing you'll be getting the right returns for investments made.

How to Know You've Identified the Right Results

How do you know you've done a good job in defining your desired results? Think of the five questions here as a quality-control check on your work. You should be able to answer yes to all five of these questions. Are you ...

1. *Better positioned to achieve your mission and vision?* These elements are not high-minded concepts that only see the light of day on special occasions. They're not reserved solely for the landing page of your company's website. Use them on a daily basis. Test them against work you're doing on issues large and small. Change must be consistent with the foundation of your organization. If you're making changes, are they aligned with your organization's ultimate aims? If yes, move forward. If no, revisit the foundations of your organization and your change work. One of them is off base.

2. *Clearer about the beliefs and values that guide your daily decisions?* The changes you desire and how you go about achieving them should be in line with the beliefs and values of your organization. Give them a careful

review. Be able to make a case for how they are guiding your change decisions. If people disagree about decisions that affect changes to be made, spend the time needed to iron out these differences. Every action you take ought to be in line with your core beliefs and values, or you shouldn't be taking it.

3. *An organization where people want to belong?* Change efforts, and the way they are conducted, ought to serve as recruitment and retention strategies. Changes undertaken should be making the organization more appealing to people who could or already do belong to it. If talent is leaving your organization because of the changes you're making, rethink the work you're doing. Good changes for the future should motivate people to want to stick around for that future.

4. *Able to better satisfy the needs of your stakeholders?* If the changes you're making are not better at meeting the needs of your stakeholders, you have a problem. A big one. Self-serving organizations don't succeed. You need to take care of the members of your organization. They're one set of your stakeholders, but far from the only one. Think bigger and broader when deciding

what needs to change to achieve the results you desire. Some stakeholder needs may be in conflict. It's your job to work through these—on your own and with these stakeholders. Sometimes you can't get everybody on the exact same page. Set yourself up for future success and communicate to stakeholders whose needs may not be fully met. Bring them into the tent and share with them the decisions you've made, and why and how you can still best serve them.

5. *More capable of making additional changes needed in the future?* Change is not a one-time deal. You've been making them since your organization began. And you're going to be making more until your organization ceases to exist. Ensure that while you're changing, you're learning how to change. Change-able organizations enjoy a competitive advantage over others. Next time you need to change course, you'll be able to do it faster, more easily, and better than other players in your markets.

Understanding Faster, Easier, Better Results through a Leverage Change Lens

The goals of Leverage Change are faster, easier, better results. No need to settle for only one or two of these advantages. You get all three from working with this new approach. Don't be seduced by quick fixes that seem to meet these goals sooner but won't serve you well later. Here's how these three benefits are defined the Leverage Change way.

Faster Results

Common sense says that if you want faster results, work on things you can finish the soonest. Want to improve your teamwork? Clarify roles and goals. Need a new strategy? Get the top team to define a path forward for the organization. But proceed with caution. In the world of Leverage Change, soonest may not always be fastest. How can that be? Think in terms of sustained change.

Your team's effectiveness might benefit immediately from a half-day session dedicated to understanding different work styles and how you can collaborate more effectively. Things get a little better for a short time, but what if your team's issues are deeper? Maybe your path to higher performance appears to be a slower one. Say your team really needs more vulnerability and to have some difficult conversations. What appears to be fastest in the near term ends up being disappointing over the longer haul. Leverage Change invites you to achieve faster results that yield positive impact immediately *and over time*.

Let's return to that strategy-setting scenario. You save time in setting strategy by having a small group of executives do the up-front work. This seemingly quicker way will leave you paying for these time savings many times over. How? With slower implementation, less commitment, and more resistance. What's the payoff from going slow to go fast by involving more people?

- Better understanding of the strategy because people have been engaged in shaping it
- More ready acceptance of needed changes
- Appreciation of why these shifts are required
- Smarter, more strategic decisions made every day by everyone
- Work done across the entire organization that supports the direction you want to be heading
- Increased commitment to making changes work

Faster results in the world of Leverage Change include both results achieved right away and those achieved over time. The bar for success is much higher in this new paradigm. Faster doesn't mean sooner. It means accomplishing sustained results that occur more rapidly than you would believe. Sometimes what appears faster in the near term turns out to be slower in the long term.

STORY

We were once working with a technology products company where this "go slow to go fast" approach paid big dividends. Even after partnering with a Japanese company to supplement its competencies, the business needed to make more changes. The senior executives decided to "clean sheet" the company's strategy going forward. That meant bringing questions, not answers, to the rest of the organization. It was an opportunity for people to develop a future they wanted to call their own. We organized a series of three 500-person meetings to work the strategy. The entire business was involved. It took four months to arrive at a set of decisions.

Investments seemed to pay off immediately. Production and quality numbers improved in the plant while we were still holding the sessions. Further benefits came when it was time for implementation. Although it took four months to develop the strategy, the organization was six months ahead of schedule when it came time to implementing it because of the high-involvement approach used. Changes were made in the organization's structure, core work processes, and culture. Two new products moved from design to manufacturing in the same time frame. The leadership team estimated that they could have developed a strategy in about a month. Their guess at implementation timing? Two years or more.

With Leverage Change, "faster" means right here and now *and* over time. Sustainability is the ultimate goal of all change work. Too often organizations achieve "rubber-band change": things appear better for a month or two, maybe even six, and then inevitably snap back to the way they have always been. Short-term results that fizzle over time aren't worth achieving in the first place. Invest early. Play the short and the long game. Adopt the Leverage Change definition of faster results.

Easier Results

Common wisdom in the world of change is to go after "low-hanging fruit" and "quick wins" early in an effort. It's the easiest work. Likely faster, too. But is it always better? The Leverage Change approach says you need to achieve all three objectives of faster, easier, and better, none at the cost of another.

As I've stated before, *don't confuse easy results with achieving needed results in easier ways.* Once you identify results that matter—both those to accomplish immediately and over time—move on to how to achieve these results more easily than you otherwise would have imagined. The question you need to ask is, "How can I make it easier to achieve results with maximum impact?" That's a strategic question. That's where the levers come into play.

Think outside the box of quick wins. These may be easy to achieve, but don't be seduced into thinking that this list of results is also better. Look beyond the obvious. Would progress in one area earn more points with the organization than a completed quick win? Convince more people you're serious? Get the organization rallying around work that matters more? Going against the grain of common wisdom may be your best bet. Give some thought to leaving the low-hanging fruit for someone else to pick. Focus on impact. Then we'll find ways by applying the 8 Levers to make it easier to bank these and other wins in your change work.

STORY

A packaged foods manufacturer was undertaking a substantial change effort. The CEO had been sending a not-so-subtle hint to his team for quite a while that emotions were not to be tolerated. Business was a rational enterprise. Numbers ruled the day. How people felt wasn't a second-class issue—it wasn't an issue at all. The CEO never acknowledged his feelings and shut conversations down when his team talked about their people's experience of the pending changes. When there was conflict in the team, the CEO avoided the issues.

The easiest work would have been to stay where the team had learned to operate: analyzing and making decisions regarding market share, product development cycle times, and retention numbers. They were well practiced and good at these things. In this situation, this work seemed to be the lowest-hanging fruit. However, the team had already been there and done these tasks.

But doing the easiest work—work that would have little impact beyond business as usual—wouldn't be worth doing at all. There were bigger issues for the team to resolve. We decided to use the Start with Impact, Follow the Energy lever. The CEO benefited from some good one-on-one coaching about the results of insisting that emotions be off-limits for the team. Some truth telling from a couple of brave direct reports helped too. They shared how they felt shut down in team meetings, how they couldn't bring the senior team fully up to speed regarding their parts of the operation without including how people felt about the pending changes.

The greatest breakthrough for the team, and ultimately for the company, would come when the CEO learned to be more vulnerable. This lesson didn't come easily to him. The Leverage Change challenge became how to make this work easier than it otherwise would have been. More information proved helpful to the CEO. He came to understand what he was giving up by priding himself on being a "numbers guy"—to the exclusion of the rest of the reality people were experiencing.

The CEO decided to take a leap of faith. There was a big backstory in his life that no one had ever heard before. Supported by some strong facilitation, he talked with the team about his past and why emotions were difficult for him to express. It got very personal. Long-ago stories of his relationship with his dad explained his behavior today. This difficult work led to much more honest and productive conversations about team dynamics than had previously been undiscussable. The CEO began to appreciate the fears that people in the organization had about planned changes. The coaching and conversations with his direct reports made addressing this issue easier. So did active facilitation in the team meeting when the issue was raised. Change can be hard. Making it easier is the value added by a Leverage Change approach.

Better Results

You may be most effective making changes in a particular part of your organization. Odds are, the smaller the change you're trying to make, the more successful you'll be in making it. Start with a pilot program where you test a change out on a small scale. Involve a small part of the organization. Resource it well. Put your best people on it. Get regular progress reports to the senior team. Shine a spotlight on the process. You'll likely succeed. But are you achieving a better result than if you had started where the work was harder?

With a pilot, you stack the deck in your favor. So much so that the scenario can sometimes bear little resemblance to how these changes will be implemented in the rest of your organization. Try to take this change work to the larger enterprise, and you won't have these same advantages. Succeeding on a small test case (read: one not tied to the scope, scale, or complexities of the day-to-day operations of the organization) will not always lead you to a better result.

Is the pilot approach the right change to be making for maximum impact? That's the Leverage Change question. Maybe you need to focus where you'll make the biggest difference even if you fall short of achieving all your objectives. It could be smarter to go where your chances of a win are lower but your payoff for victory higher.

This is not a flat-out argument against pilots. Leverage Change contends that you need to consider your options carefully. What are the trade-offs between a near-certain win on a small scale versus a tougher challenge—but a probably more high-impact effort—on a large scale? What appears obvious on the surface may not be as clear with a closer look. The best results for an organization most often come in the form of doing the most important work.

STORY

Jennifer Brown, a diversity, equity, and inclusion (DEI) consultant, and her colleagues once worked with a company that licensed its software on a subscription basis, hosting the platform centrally on the web. The CEO had made it his personal mission to fix the gender pay gap at the business after an internal assessment uncovered a marked disparity between men and women.

Brown worked with him as he considered the trade-offs between piloting a program on a small scale and making sweeping changes across the entire organization all at once. On the basis of his own deep commitment, the difference it would make for his female employees, and the message it would send to the rest of the organization, he decided that the change needed to be made company-wide from the start.

By investing millions of dollars and taking decisive action, the CEO guaranteed fair treatment for all female employees, immediately and into the future. He also ensured that his equal-pay initiative wouldn't be a quick fix. It would remain both a challenge and an opportunity that required revisiting every year. The commitment to equal pay for equal work was going to stay solid, regardless of the company's performance or market fluctuations. That's how he defined better results and maximum impact on this important issue—for him and the organization.

Some Final Tips and Advice in Defining Desired Results

We've covered a lot of ground regarding results so far. Here are a few final thoughts to consider:

1. *Know your reality.* Start where you are. Take honest stock of your current circumstances. This activity can be quite comprehensive, such as an organization-wide assessment of key functions' performance against plan. For example, in what areas are you succeeding, and why are you're winning in these areas? Where are you falling short, and what reasons can explain these shortfalls?

   Depending on your situation, it can be just as valuable to take a more straightforward approach. I've worked with clients to list operating core processes underlying how work gets done (e.g., communications, decision-making, rewards, etc.). Once you define these core elements, you can create simple but powerful lists of what's been working and what hasn't in the business.

You decide how formal and involved this assessment needs to be. Either path can get you where you want to go. Which feels most appropriate for the work you're undertaking? Bottom line, you can't set good results for your future if you don't know the position from which you're beginning.

2. *Consider defining results in different ways.* Most people doing change work pay mind to only one of four kinds of potential results: the numbers. We're obsessed with needing to count things to measure success. Defects per thousand items. Return on fixed assets. Percentage of market share. All important and valid measures—just not the only kind that count. Here are three others to consider when defining desired results:

    • *What you see.* How are different parts of the organization working together? Can you see greater collaboration in problem-solving activities between functions that used to be at odds? Are new skills that were learned in development programs being applied on the job? Are people showing up for meetings that they used to avoid like the plague because the meetings are now more positive and productive?

• *What you hear.* Customer feedback, both through formal surveys and informal talks, counts. Add to this list the kinds of questions people ask in town hall meetings. What kind of quality and depth of conversations are you hearing when teams get together? Are interactions between bosses and subordinates filled with offers of support that help people keep their commitments?

• *What you feel.* Do you personally feel that there is trust and vulnerability on your team? (Yes, our own feelings count too.) How confident are people feeling about the path being crafted to reach their collective future? How much alignment do we feel that we have among the executive team around our new strategy?

Too often these three types of results get forgotten when organizations define success. All four types are valid. Get a complete picture by not forgetting any of them.

3. *Create as clear, as comprehensive, and as compelling a picture of your future as possible.* Get real about your future. As real as possible. Make the picture of your future so detailed and realistic that you can imagine stepping into and living it. It accounts for your markets, competitors, issues, and opportunities. Don't forget to take a look inside your organization at your people, processes, and practices.
   • How is work getting done?
   • What products and services are you providing?
   • Who is in this future with you?
   • How are you and they behaving?
   • What decisions do you see yourself making and why?

   Be clear about where you're headed. Define as much detail as you can muster. Fill out the entire canvas on which you're painting. Leave no corner untouched.

4. *Engage as many of the interested and affected parties as you can.* It will always feel easier to close ranks and keep things "under control." But engagement, not manageability, is the goal. Think beyond the usual suspects. Invite someone from the frontlines to join you in defining the best results for your change work. Don't shy away from

partnering with customers who will benefit from changes you make. Think about inviting people two or three levels above or below you in the organization's hierarchy to get involved. Videoconference folks in from the other side of the world. Assign everyone involved in the change work the task of talking to stakeholders and finding out what matters to them. What do they care about most? What are their greatest concerns? hopes? fears? Let go a little so that others can gain a better grip on the work.

5. *Don't undersell yourself.* Now is the time for bold moves. Go big or stay home. Most of the work in organizations on results makes this harder. SMART goals have a huge following in the world of individual, team, and organization change. SMART stands for **s**pecific, **m**easurable, **a**chievable, **r**ealistic, and **t**ime-bound.

There's only one problem with this approach.

It puts you on a path of achieving nothing more than incremental improvements—they're achievable and realistic. Don't get carried away with anything too brash! SMART goals almost shout from the mountaintops to stay in your box. Here's a different way to look at defining results. Thanks to work by Mark Murphy, we can expand the possibilities of desired results.[20] He calls them HARD goals. HARD stands for

• **H**eartfelt. You deeply care about the goal you are working on. It has profound meaning and power for you.

• **A**nimated. Your goal brings you energy. No matter how big an ask it may be, it energizes you to take a major step forward.

• **R**equired. These are nonnegotiable results. Other people are counting on you to deliver, to make good on your promises to them. Much more than action plans, these are agreements entered into with real commitment.

• **D**ifficult. Your goals should be a reach, an honest stretch for you and your organization. Don't settle for small improvements. Challenge yourself to bring your best and more to the table.

You're going to be investing in any change work you're doing. Make sure that at the end of the day, you're delighted with what you've accomplished. That feeling of a big win starts with how you define the goals or results you're aiming to achieve.

Don't try to bring about change the way that those who lost to Archimedes did. Working harder without leverage is no way to go through life. Approaching change this way is more difficult, will take more time, and is less effective. Consider your situation. Get crystal clear on the results you need to achieve. Make sure they're the right results for you to achieve. Learn which of the 8 Levers will make the biggest difference first. Start with those. Learn the others. Get good at using all eight, any place and at any time.

10

TAKING LEVERAGE INTO YOUR OWN HANDS

Now that you've read of the power and possibilities of the 8 Levers, let's revisit the value of leverage, which I first described in the introduction.

Reframing "Do More with Less"

The 8 Levers are designed to make your work with change better by any measure. By applying the levers, you can't help but have your efforts become easier at the same time. The more you take advantage of the levers, the faster your organization will move into the future.

"Do more with less." The dirty words of organization change. People hear them and run for cover. (It's akin to saying to someone, "I have some feedback for you." The other party braces themselves. Maybe it means you're going to give them a raise. Likely not.) Through years of conditioning, we've learned to cringe when the words come up. They usually mean bad news. Last time you told someone to do more with less, you may have been announcing a downsizing. Maybe a group inherited more work that came along with a new IT solution. Perhaps your customers were demanding more benefits regarding quality, cost, or timing. The situation doesn't matter. The equation is always the same: expectations up, resources down. You've played this game before. There are no winners, only losers. The lucky ones are still around to tell tales of before and after the magic statement was made.

I hope that after reading this book you've been able to reframe those "dirty words" into a fresh perspective on change. See how much leverage you can create in your change work. Challenge yourself to see how big an impact you can create with less arguing with "resisters," less getting locked into using someone else's model for your change effort when you'll be better adapting it or creating your own, less discounting the value of everyone in your organization when it comes to being smart about the business. Doing more with less means accomplishing more with less unnecessary Or debates, less time waiting to see results, less of the "What's in it for me?" stage of change work. Doing more with less, the right kinds of less, becomes a goal. The levers are designed to meet those needs. They have been tested in organizations of all types, with all kinds of changes, at all stages of change efforts, by all manner of people. The specifics don't matter. The levers will add value for you and others. Use them a little and your organization will benefit. Use them a lot and expect more.

A Quick Primer on Pulling the Right Levers

Working smarter not harder with the levers means knowing how to use every one of them at any time. The more of them you're capable of using, the more flexibility you'll have and the more successful you'll be. Before you begin a change task, pause. Reflect. The common problems with change and the associated levers were identified at the beginning of each chapter. (These are summarized in table 10.1.) The levers don't remove work from the change equation. Instead, they shift the kind of work that needs to be done and make it more productive.

Compare these lists to your current situation. Think through which levers make the most sense for you to focus on right now. Use the following questions as your guide:

- Which common problems listed in the table are most present in your change challenge?
- Which lever(s) will give you the biggest leg up in achieving faster, easier, better results?

TABLE 10.1 Common Problems and the Levers That Address Them

COMMON PROBLEM	LEVER THAT ADDRESSES IT
There's too much change.	Pay Attention to Continuity
Change takes too long.	Think and Act as If the Future Were Now!
People reject your change approach because it's "Not Invented Here."	Design It Yourself
People don't know enough to make good decisions.	Create a Common Database
All change efforts must begin from the top.	Start with Impact, Follow the Energy
So many ask "What's in it for me?"	Develop a Future People Want to Call Their Own
People get to do only the routine work of their regular job.	Find Opportunities for People to Make a Meaningful Difference
People's plates are already full.	Make Change Work Part of Daily Work

The common problems provide a road map for you in identifying which levers to put into play first. The levers trigger ideas for actions you could take. Where are there opportunities for impact in the organization? Where do you have energy to begin? Sometimes answers to these questions will appear in neon before you. At other times you'll need to dig below the surface to uncover clues and put a larger puzzle together.

Working with the levers is likely to be a different approach than you're used to. It's a little art and a bit of science. Gather information and make a judgment call about what you think is missing in the situation. Trust your gut. Applying a lever won't hurt you. You can do no wrong. The only question: Can you do more right?

Levers Your Organization Can Apply

Each of the 8 Levers is going to fall into one of the following three categories for your organization. Which lever(s) you choose to apply first in your situation should be a combination of the one or more that you can use most effectively and those that will give you the greatest positive impact. The groupings here can help you make these decisions.

These Levers Are Part of Your Culture

These are the easy ones. They're in your DNA. They are naturally the way people think and act—and have for as far back as anyone can remember. You can tell that levers fall into this bucket when you point out someone using one in the business and they don't know what you're talking about. The organization has unconscious competence. No extra effort is required to remember to take advantage of these levers.

Knowing what these are, though, can make you more aware of when to best apply them. When new people join your organization, educate them about these core competencies. Don't make them have to find out on their own through trial and error. When you work with other organizations, point these strengths out to them and make yourself a more appealing partner.

STORY

A mining company I worked with was always focused on the future. The leader read futurist books and magazines. He studied the art of invention and was obsessed with, as he put it, "Translating thought into action." He embedded into the culture of his organization the lever Think and Act as If the Future Were Now! He did it himself all the time, rewarded people for doing it, and called special attention to it in meetings. He asked me to design experiences for teams in his business so that they could time-travel into the future and look back at innovations they had integrated into their daily operations. He shared his own strong suit with everyone in the organization, teaching them to apply a powerful lever to advantage. Over time, it became a part of the way the organization operated.

You've Learned to Apply the Levers from Past Change Work

You haven't come by these levers naturally. You've had to work at them. Sometime in the past you needed to make use of these levers and learned their value. They worked for you, and you used them again and again until you became proficient at wielding them.

STORY

The CEO of a building products company was moving on in her career. The first order of business for the new operations team was overseeing a major overhaul of the company's information systems. New business processes and practices needed to accompany the renovated IT system. The change was going to impact every person in the company. It was a nearly all-consuming task. But the new CEO had watched his mentor lead the business for years. He had taken notes on what he thought worked well about her style of leading, and what didn't. She was a savant at knowing when to provide direction and when to encourage others in the business to participate, but this skill wasn't passed on to the organization.

Despite the pressing needs related to implementing the IT system upgrade, the new CEO dedicated time to the Pay Attention to Continuity lever. When it came time for the new CEO to take the reins, he knew there were areas where he needed to up his game. Leveraging the direction/participation polarity was an area that he needed to attend to for himself—and for the entire operation. Although the organization had had a great model for a long time in the prior CEO, this lever was one that had to be developed in the rest of the organization from the ground up. As time went on, everyone in the business got better at discerning when direction was needed, and when participation would serve them better. But it was a learned skill, not something inherited along with the culture.

You've Never Applied These Levers Before

These are the toughest levers to make part of your daily organizational life. You begin with no competence in them. You may not even have realized that they existed before you read about them in this book. To begin, you first need to know that this particular lever will help in your current situation. Second, you'll need to be able to explain to others why it will be helpful. Finally, you and they will need to understand how to apply it.

STORY

A technology company faced the challenge of needing to rapidly educate its entire workforce about its financial standing. Money was tight, and people needed to understand why, and what they could do about it. It was an all-hands-on-deck situation. Business as usual was to operate in silos. You stick to your job; I'll stick to mine. Dealing effectively with coming budget cuts was going to take working together in new ways. Cross-departmental teams were set up. Organization-wide events were held. For a solid six months, as much energy was devoted to thinking and acting as a single team as there was to getting product out the door to each business unit's customers. Compared to how the organization had done business in the past, this type of one-team behavior was as different as night and day.

A new lever was in play: Create a Common Database. Without it the organization never would have made the budget numbers.

A lot of support and structure was needed to help bring this lever to life. New behavior led to new results, however, and as people began to change their behavior, the organization as a whole increased its competence with using this lever.

Being Strategic about the Levers You Pull

Here's a challenge for you. Which levers would you pull first in the next story, and why? There are no wrong answers, so your strategic moves may be as good as mine. Remember, you don't need to pull many levers as you decide which will serve you best in the story. You may decide to use only one to begin and then assess its influence before moving on. Focus on maximum impact in deciding which levers deserve special attention. Which will give you the biggest ROI? What resources do you have available? Where would it be wisest to devote them?

STORY

The international HR arm of a global entertainment company was challenged by the need to improve relationships with managers in the businesses that they served. Things hadn't been terrible, but they could be better. Some of the issues were attributed to a new organization structure that still needed a few kinks ironed out. Other problems were chalked up to personality clashes. Most were explained by unclear roles and expectations among all players. Who was responsible for what? What could they each count on from one another? The senior leader of the HR team was new. Uncertain of the best way forward, she was hesitant to alienate the HR group's new clients. At the same time, she had an equal concern about frustrating her new team.

Speed was an issue, as the new organization structure was already up and running. To everyone else, the old centralized shared-services model was a dim and distant memory. Business unit leaders wanted their HR work done, and done now. The change drum had been beating ever louder throughout the enterprise as moves by competitors launching innovative business lines were eating into profit margins. The HR business partners wanted to do right by their new clients. At the same time, they were uncertain about what *right* looked like. Was it even the same picture for everyone involved? If they had to customize services for different businesses too much, would it lead to more headaches from not being able to coordinate systems and processes among themselves?

Functional and business leaders had to get on the same page. The entire HR organization needed to operate as one team. HR consultants met with their respective business-line customers, shared expectations, and reached tentative agreements on how they would work together. The HR people met back as a whole team to compare notes, accept agreements that worked for all, and modify those that didn't. A series of conversations between HR team members and line managers led to a list of joint commitments. Doing this type of negotiating wasn't a natural ability in the organization. It needed to become a learned skill, improved through practice. Eventually, this new competency was used by the organization more and more.

In the situation I've described here, I was most intrigued by the following levers, and here's why:

- *Pay Attention to Continuity.* There were major changes under way in this organization, both between the HR team and their business-line clients, and within the HR team itself. The question of needing to coordinate systems and processes among themselves caught my eye. Dealing with both internal and external change is a big challenge and can lead to a good deal of conflict. But what about continuity? We heard little about this in the scenario here, so that was a clue that continuity might deserve more time and attention going forward.

- *Think and Act as If the Future Were Now!* Speed was important. That was clearly called out by the business-line leaders. These clients' impatience was noted, yet it had not been accounted for. The rest of the organization was proceeding forward with the reorganization. If the HR team didn't get a move on, they would be stuck in a reactive mode from which they might never recover.
- *Develop a Future You Would Be Proud to Call Your Own.* There were a number of stakeholders, each with powerful drivers to get their own needs met. They also had little interest in collaborating with one another, more motivated by impacts the changes would have on them individually. The direct line relationship was between the HR business partners and their line leaders. Allegiance to

the HR organization was coming in second place in a two-team race. A picture of a common future, one that worked for all, seemed to be missing in this scenario. Building that shared vision would be helpful to all stakeholders, and they'd all need to have a hand in doing so for it to work.

- *Find Opportunities for People to Make a Meaningful Difference.* Many people were struggling with this change, so I wondered where there were opportunities for people to make meaningful differences. That led me to zero in on questions around decision-making, such as these:

    • Who would be involved in making the final operational decisions, and how?

    • How much say would the clients have in developing the solution?

    • Would the different clients agree with one another on the resulting responses?

    • In what ways would the new leader's indecisiveness play out over time?

    These questions of involvement would be central to the answers about roles and responsibilities. Knowing who was going to be involved in determining how the HR group would move forward, how, and when would be a high-leverage area to focus attention.

Where was your attention drawn in this case? Which levers spoke to you loudest about needing attention? Where did you see leverage?

This quick primer was intended to get you thinking about the levers as a whole set of eight, not just individually. You may have noticed the paradox that the more levers you pull, the greater the leverage you have *and* the harder it is to pay attention to those you have pulled!

Tips and Advice for Pulling Each Lever

As you think about pulling each of the 8 Levers, pay attention to the success factors described in the earlier chapters.

PAY ATTENTION TO CONTINUITY

- Adopt a paradoxical point of view about change.
- Believe that there is wisdom in resistance.
- Commit to listening to the fewer and less powerful.
- See those resisting change as key contributors, not troublemakers.
- Know that you're all on the same team.

THINK AND ACT AS IF THE FUTURE WERE NOW!

- Embrace this new paradigm.
- Envision a winning future.
- Get more people asking the question, "If we were in our preferred future, how would we approach this situation?"
- Fail fast, learn, and improve.
- Communicate lessons learned, far and wide.

DESIGN IT YOURSELF

- Get the right people involved from the start.
- Learn from your organization's past experiences with change.
- Get your arms around as much of the mess as you can.
- Creatively expand what you think you know.
- Define a clear purpose and outcomes.
- Develop a road map that will achieve your purpose and outcomes.
- Check your plans and change them as needed.

CREATE A COMMON DATABASE

- Include both internal and external information.
- Pay attention to both facts and feelings.

- Put processes in place for sustaining learning over time.
- Learn how to communicate effectively through both inquiry and advocacy.
- Pay attention to different perspectives on the same information.

START WITH IMPACT, FOLLOW THE ENERGY

- Have your finger on the pulse of the organization.
- Do the work that needs to be done—not always the work you planned to do.
- Make sure that leadership is willing to trust the process.
- Be opportunistic and planful.
- Don't let your own agenda be (the only) driver in the process.

DEVELOP A FUTURE PEOPLE WANT TO CALL THEIR OWN

- Identify collaborators for an ideal future.
- Engage your stakeholders in ways they will want to engage with you.
- Persevere it will serve you well
- Get creative by gaining a new perspective.
- Give yourself permission to get it wrong.

FIND OPPORTUNITIES FOR PEOPLE TO MAKE A MEANINGFUL DIFFERENCE

- Find the best way for people to make a difference in your organization.
- Gain agreement from key stakeholders about who decides what and the difference that can make.
- Discover new ways to involve people.
- Worry less about having what you say count.
- Get people focused on making a difference for everyone.

MAKE CHANGE WORK PART OF DAILY WORK

- See change as everybody's job.
- Coordinate around common goals.
- Define clear measures of success.
- Ensure everyone has the freedom to make needed changes.
- Be certain you are capable of making needed changes.

Some Final Counsel

The 8 Levers are a gift that keeps on giving. Use them, and you can achieve results faster, more easily, and better than ever before. The more you use the levers, the more gains you'll claim. They are designed to be applied to any change, anywhere, at any time, and by anyone. They are twenty-first-century competencies for organizations and their members, an equal-opportunity value add whether the decisions you're making will impact an entire organization, a community, a team, or just your own work. They are guides for both your mindset and your behavior. Change either and you can change both, and in doing so, you will make the world a better place in which you and others work and live.

Where do you go from here? A few final tips and advice.

Think Big

Applying the levers can lead to extraordinary gains, far greater than you may have imagined before. Don't set your bar too low. What before seemed like too big a stretch is now within your reach. Shorten a two-year project timeline to six months. Aim for 50 percent improvement in quality instead of an incremental 10 percent year over year. Take 75 percent of the market in a new niche you develop. "Unrealistic" expectations lead to extraordinary achievements. Don't settle for really good when exceptional is possible. Test different levers in the same situation. Some will pay off more than others. Stick with those and save the others for another day.

Partner with Others

You're not going to get this job done alone. You never were going to. The levers you find most challenging, others find easy. And vice versa. Find these people. Work with them. Learn from them. Ask for their advice about which levers they believe will best serve you in your current situation. All eight will be helpful. Others can help you decide where your own 80-20 rule lies. Pareto's principle says that applying the right 20 percent of the levers will give you 80 percent of the benefit. Think together about what makes the most sense. These new partners can also support you in applying the levers you select. The name of the game is teamwork.

Be Confident with Risk

Working with the levers is not without risk. If you want a safer path, look for more linear ways to get from point A to point B. Leverage means making bets, on yourself and others. You can't be certain of outcomes. You wouldn't have picked up this book if you were satisfied with the status quo. Fortune favors the bold. The more you work with the levers, the better they'll work for you.

Improve Whatever Change Work You're Already Making

The levers don't restrict any of the change work you're doing already. They supplement what's good and improve what needs additional support. Adopt an attitude that the levers will aid your efforts, and you'll be surprised by the opportunities you see for improving your change work. If one lever's not working for you, try another. They are designed to work together and apart. You'll know when great things are happening.

It's about a Better Way, Not the Right Way

Remember that at the end of the day, the levers are not about the one best way. With the levers, everyone wins. Are you accomplishing results faster? Is accomplishing them easier? Is the quality of the changes you're making better? The more you use the levers, the more benefit you'll receive. Find your path. And move your world!

NOTES

[1]   Stuart A. Kauffman, *At Home in the Universe: The Search for the Laws of Self-Organization and Complexity* (New York: Oxford University Press, 1995).

[2]   Barry Johnson, *Polarity Management: Identifying and Managing Unsolvable Problems* (Amherst, MA: HRD Press, 1992).

[3]   Barry Johnson, *And: Making a Difference by Leveraging Polarity, Paradox or Dilemma*, vol.1 (Amherst, MA: HRD Press, 2020).

[4]   Richard H. Axelrod, Emily Axelrod, Julie Beedon, and Robert W. Jake Jacobs, *You Don't Have to Do It Alone: How to Involve Others to Get Things Done* (Oakland, CA: Berrett-Koehler, 2004), 54.

[5]   Johnson, *And*, 104.

[6]   Mirjana R. Gearhart, "FORUM: John A. Wheeler: From the Big Bang to the Big Crunch," Cosmic Search 1 (4), http://www.bigear.org/vol1no4/wheeler.htm.

[7]   Stanley M. Davis, *Future Perfect* (New York: Basic Books, 1987).

[8]   Peter Block, *The Empowered Manager: Positive Political Skills at Work* (San Francisco: Jossey-Bass, 1987).

[9]   Peter Drucker, *The Practice of Management* (New York: Harper & Row, 1954).

[10]   Michele Gelfand, Sarah Gordon, Chengguang Li, Virginia Choi, and Piotr Prokopowicz, "One Reason Mergers Fail: The Two Cultures Aren't Compatible," *Harvard Business Review*, October 2, 2018.

[11]   Ken Blanchard and Jesse Stoner, *Full Steam Ahead! Unleash the Power of Vision in Your Work and Your Life* (Oakland, CA: Berrett-Koehler, 2004).

[12]   Marilee Adams, *Change Your Questions, Change Your Life: 10 Powerful Tools for Life and Work* (Oakland, CA: Berrett-Koehler, 2009).

[13]   Jay Galbraith, *Organization Design* (Reading, MA: Addison-Wesley, 1977).

[14]   Randy L. Albert, Kathleen D. Dannemiller, Roland J. Loup, and Robert W. Jacobs, *Interactive Strategic Planning: A Consultant's Guide* (Ann Arbor, MI: Dannemiller Tyson Associates, 1990).

[15]   Daniel Goleman, *Emotional Intelligence: Why It Can Matter More Than IQ* (New York: Bantam, 2005).

[16]   Ron Lippitt, *The Dynamics of Planned Change: A Comparative Study of Principles and Techniques* (New York: Harcourt Brace, 1958).

[17]   Randy Albert, Kathleen Dannemiller, Robert Jacobs, and Roland Loup, *Interactive Strategic Planning* (Ann Arbor, MI: Dannemiller Tyson Associations, 1996).

[18]   Attributed to Kurt Lewin in Charles W. Tolman, Frances Cherry, Rene van Herzewijk, and Ian Lubek (Eds.), *Problems of Theoretical Psychology* (North York, ON: Captus University Publications, 1995), 31.

[19]   Peter Block, *Community: The Structure of Belonging* (Oakland, CA: Berrett-Koehler, 2009).

[20]   Mark Murphy, *Hard Goals: The Secret to Getting from Where You Are to Where You Want to Be* (New York: McGraw-Hill Education, 2010).

ACKNOWLEDGMENTS

I wrote this book alone in my home office, yet I experienced the partnership of so many throughout the process.

First and foremost, I am grateful to the people in organizations around the world who have given me the privilege of serving them. The lessons I learned appear throughout these pages.

Next, thank you to Jesse Stoner, without whom this book would not have been written. She has been a good friend and colleague for more than twenty-five years and suggested I write it. She also challenged my thinking, celebrated insights I discovered, and helped me capture on these pages what I have come to believe about the world of change.

My work with Mark Hurwich began before any of my writing on the book started. He guided me in envisioning the project as an easy, rapid, enjoyable experience. That's just what it's been. Mark Levy has been my writing coach for years. The shorter sentences and easier reading in the book are thanks to him. My mom and dad are next in line, as they consistently checked on my progress, could always tell you which chapter I was working on, and had an encouraging word that the end was in sight.

My nephew Alex Jacobs was the first to read the entire manuscript, suggested useful ideas, and provided the first test of whether my baby was ugly or not. Robert Bogue, Lori Roth, and Chloe Lizotte each reviewed the manuscript. Their feedback helped me write a better, clearer book. Thanks as well to Michael Sprague and Zack Robertson, clients and colleagues who put their oars in the water when I needed to test whether what I was writing would make sense to others.

What can one say about my editor Steve Piersanti? This is the third book I've had the honor of working on with Steve. While deriving what felt like a certain devious satisfaction from sending me back to the drawing board a few times, he offered wise, patient, and enlightening counsel. He helped me bring my best self to the book. The email he sent me saying "Outstanding! This is looking good!" has been bestowed a place on my refrigerator.

I hit the jackpot twenty-nine years ago when Berrett-Koehler agreed to publish my first book, *Real Time Strategic Change*. BK is a special group of people whose partnership I felt every step of the way in bringing these ideas to you.

I have worked with and learned from Barry Johnson for more than twenty-five years. His wisdom is featured in the first chapter of the book on paradoxical change, and his influence helped shape portions of other chapters as well. Kathie Dannemiller, my first mentor, taught me so much about organizations and how to help them achieve their preferred futures. She was with me in spirit throughout my writing.

The many colleagues (who double as friends) whom I've worked with over the years have also been teachers for me. What I've gained from these relationships has significantly shaped what I have shared with you.

The cover design graphic by Rob Johnson has captured the power and possibilities the concept of leverage has for people in organizations to move their worlds. My production manager, Susan Geraghty, made pulling together all the pieces and parts of the book an easy and flawless process. Michele Jones's copyediting went beyond grammar and punctuation—what you've read is better for her expert touch.

The book would not be complete without a thank you to Theo, my informal coauthor and companion, who lay next to me patiently waiting for his daily walk that conveniently coincided with my need for a break from writing for the day.

Finally, a thank you to Amy for everything. She lovingly responded to my seemingly endless string of "What about if I said's," "Would it sound better if I wrote it this way's," and "Could you tell me what you think's." She read and reread drafts, celebrated progress and accomplishments, and consoled me when I was stuck. She also gracefully created space in the rest of our life for my writing time.

ABOUT THE AUTHOR

Photo by Michael Nemeth

Why do some organizations work and others don't? **Robert W. Jake Jacobs** has been curious about that question since his first real job on the assembly line of an ice cream novelty manufacturing plant making bomb pops and push-up bars.

Spurred by this same question and wanting to leverage his expertise gained by tending bar, he crafted his undergraduate honors thesis, *Bars in a College Town*. His first publication, in the *Pittsburgh Undergraduate Review*, described the positive results achieved through a custom-made curriculum and teaching style he invented to support a child with a learning disability.

As a pioneer in the field of large group interventions, Jake continued his discoveries of better ways for people and organizations to change. He's worked with some of the largest corporations in the world, including Corning, Ford, Marriott, and TJMaxx. He has also supported major change efforts with the City of New York, the US Forest Service, the US Environmental Protection Agency, and the United Kingdom's National Health and Employment Services. The Illumination Project, of which he is founder and CEO, has created unique opportunities for some of the most important work in his career: further strengthening citizen–police relationships with trust and legitimacy.

For some odd reason, Jake is drawn to big, messy, complex situations filled with multiple stakeholders that have some common, but often competing, needs. He enjoys these high-risk, high-payoff challenges while doing his best to avoid mundane projects where he'd likely create more mischief than good.

Writing has been a great way for him to get clear about what he believes. He's done so in two earlier books, *Real Time Strategic Change* and *You Don't Have to Do It Alone* (cowritten with Richard H. Axelrod, Emily Axelrod, and Julie Beedon). He has also published articles in *Strategy and Leadership*, *Executive Excellence*, *Leader to Leader*, *Strategic HR Review*, the *OD Practitioner*, and *Consulting to Management*, and has been featured in the *Huffington Post* and *Inc.* magazine.

Being adjunct faculty in Notre Dame's Executive Education Program, the US Navy's

Postgraduate Institute, Roffey Park Management Institute in England, St. Thomas University, and numerous organizations have all been opportunities to continue his own learning while teaching others.

He also readily contributes his consulting expertise to local arts organizations and nonprofit groups of all types, committed to bringing stronger, healthier communities to our world.

He now calls Toledo, Ohio, home once again, having returned after thirty years away. He spends his free time sharing meals with his parents, discovering new dining spots, traveling, cooking (especially with just a few errant ingredients in the house), living a healthy lifestyle, focusing on personal growth, listening to a wide assortment of music, and taking hikes with his best friend, Theo, an energetic hundred-pound black lab. He lives with his partner-in-everything, Amy, who brings love, fun, inspiration, challenge, and support to his life every day. He's very proud of his two grown children, Alison and Aaron, who both live in Los Angeles.

Jake can be reached at jakejacobsconsulting. com. Contact Jake about his keynotes, coaching, consulting, workshops, webinars, and training programs.

Berrett-Koehler Discussion Guide

Leverage Change

8 Ways to Achieve Faster, Easier, Better Results
Robert W. Jake Jacobs

The purpose of this book is to make great things happen with change for individuals, teams, and organizations. *Leverage Change* is both a mindset and a guide for action. Apply the 8 Levers, and you will achieve faster, easier, and better results than you imagined with any kind of change—at any time in any place by anyone. This discussion guide has been designed to help you and others deepen your understanding of *Leverage Change* and how to take advantage of the benefits it offers. You can use these questions for individual reflection, conversations with your work colleagues or a reading group, agenda items for a team dedicated to an organization change effort, or exploration with a coach or consultant. The guide is divided into three sections:

- Better understanding the levers and how to apply them
- Identifying opportunities where you can apply the levers
- Developing plans to apply the levers that will make the biggest difference for you

Better Understanding the Levers

Begin by asking these questions:

1. Which levers will be the easiest for you to use and why?
2. Which levers may be the most challenging to apply and why?
3. Which levers are already part of the way your organization, your team, or you have always thought and acted? What are some examples of how you've applied these levers in the past? What difference did they make?
4. Which levers have you learned to apply from past change work? Why were these levers needed, and how were they applied? What value did they add?
5. Which levers have you never applied before? Identify a change you've worked on in the past. What impact could you have achieved by applying one or more of the levers?

Identifying Opportunities

Here are some questions you can use to identify opportunities to apply the levers:

1. What changes are already underway in your organization or team or in your own work? For each situation, ask these questions:

- What progress, if any, has already been made?
- What issues, if any, are being experienced?
- Who is currently involved in the work and how?
2. What new changes are needed in your organization or team or in your own work? For each change, ask these questions:
- How would you know you were successful in your efforts?
- Which people could make a real difference if they were involved in this work?
- What opportunities and challenges can you imagine experiencing as you move forward with these initiatives?

Applying the Levers

Select one or more of the situations you listed in the "Identifying Opportunities" section. For each situation, do the following:
1. Choose the lever(s) to apply:
- Which of the common problems identified at the beginning of the lever chapters are your organization, your team, or you experiencing now?

- Which lever(s) will give you the biggest leg up in achieving faster, easier, and better results?

2. Identify the success factors for each lever that are already in place in your situation.

- For any that are missing, how can you ensure that you have them covered?

3. Decide how to best apply the lever(s):

- What actions can you take in line with the levers you've selected?

- Who can support your efforts?

To learn more about Leverage Change *and Robert W. Jake Jacobs, visit* www.jakejacobsconsulting.com.

Also by the author
Real Time Strategic Change

How to Involve an Entire Organization in Fast
and Far-Reaching Change

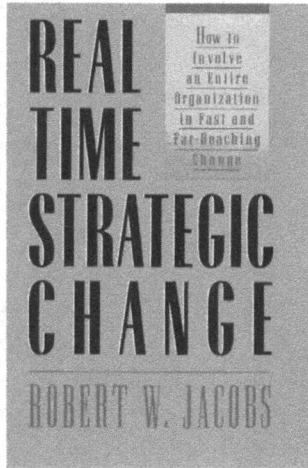

The most successful organizations of the future will be those that are capable of rapidly and effectively bringing about fundamental, lasting, system-wide changes. In response to this challenge, *Real Time Strategic Change* advocates a fundamental redesign of the way organizations change. The result is an approach that involves an entire organization in fast and far-reaching change. Complete with conceptual frameworks, tools and techniques, agendas, and roles key actors need to play, this is the first book published on this powerful approach to organizational change.

Also by the author
You Don't Have to Do It Alone
How to Involve Others to Get Things Done

By Richard H. Axelrod, Emily M. Axelrod, Julie Beedon, and Robert W. Jacobs

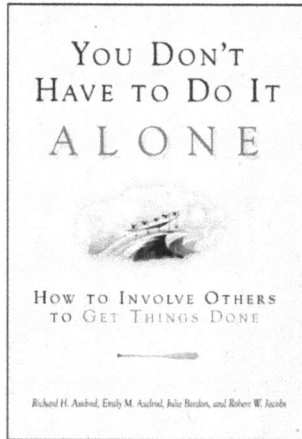

We all need to involve other people to accomplish our tasks and achieve our goals. This book lays out a simple, straightforward plan of action for finding the right people and keeping them energized, enthusiastic, and committed until the work is completed. *You Don't Have to Do It Alone* is organized around a series of five questions corresponding to steps in the involvement process. This book teaches readers to involve others in a way that will actually make work easier, resulting in less stress, better ideas, and more successful outcomes.

BK Berrett–Koehler Publishers, Inc.
www.bkconnection.com

800.929.2929

✺ Berrett–Koehler
B̅K̅ Publishers

Berrett-Koehler is an independent publisher dedicated to an ambitious mission: *Connecting people and ideas to create a world that works for all.*

Our publications span many formats, including print, digital, audio, and video. We also offer online resources, training, and gatherings. And we will continue expanding our products and services to advance our mission.

We believe that the solutions to the world's problems will come from all of us, working at all levels: in our society, in our organizations, and in our own lives. Our publications and resources offer pathways to creating a more just, equitable, and sustainable society. They help people make their organizations more humane, democratic, diverse, and effective (and we don't think there's any contradiction there). And they guide people in creating positive change in their own lives and aligning their personal practices with their aspirations for a better world.

And we strive to practice what we preach through what we call "The BK Way." At the core of this approach is *stewardship,* a deep sense of responsibility to administer the company for the benefit of all of our stakeholder groups, including authors, customers, employees, investors, service providers, sales partners, and the communities and environment around us. Everything we do is built around stewardship and our other core values of *quality, partnership, inclusion,* and *sustainability.*

This is why Berrett-Koehler is the first book publishing company to be both a B Corporation (a rigorous certification) and a benefit corporation (a for-profit legal status), which together require us to adhere to the highest standards for corporate, social, and environmental performance. And it is why we have instituted many pioneering practices (which you can learn about at www.bk connection.com), including the Berrett-Koehler Constitution, the Bill of Rights and Responsibilities for BK Authors, and our unique Author Days.

We are grateful to our readers, authors, and other friends who are supporting our mission. We ask you to share with us examples of how BK publications and resources are making a difference in your lives, organizations, and communities at www.bkconnection.com/impact.

Dear reader,

Thank you for picking up this book and welcome to the worldwide BK community! You're joining a special group of people who have come together to create positive change in their lives, organizations, and communities.

What's BK all about?

Our mission is to connect people and ideas to create a world that works for all.

Why? Our communities, organizations, and lives get bogged down by old paradigms of self-interest, exclusion, hierarchy, and privilege. But we believe that can change. That's why we seek the leading experts on these challenges—and share their actionable ideas with you.

A welcome gift

To help you get started, we'd like to offer you a **free copy** of one of our bestselling ebooks:

www.bkconnection.com/welcome

When you claim your **free ebook,** you'll also be subscribed to our blog.

Our freshest insights

Access the best new tools and ideas for leaders at all levels on our blog at ideas.bkconnection.com.

Sincerely,

Your friends at Berrett-Koehler

Certified

B

Corporation

www.ingramcontent.com/pod-product-compliance
Lightning Source LLC
Chambersburg PA
CBHW011303210326
41599CB00036B/7099